Letters on International Copyright

HENRY CHARLES CAREY

New York 1868

TABLE OF CONTENTS

PREFACE
LETTERS ON INTERNATIONAL COPYRIGHT
NOTE

PREFACE

At the date, now fourteen years since, of the first publication of these letters, the important case of authors versus readers—makers of books versus consumers of facts and ideas—had for several years been again on trial in the high court of the people. But few years previously the same plaintiffs had obtained a verdict giving large extension of time to the monopoly privileges they had so long enjoyed. Not content therewith, they now claimed greater space, desiring to have those privileges so extended as to include within their domain the vast population of the British Empire. To that hour no one had appeared before the court on the part of the defendants, prepared seriously to question the plaintiffs' assertion to the effect that literary property stood on the same precise footing, and as much demanded perpetual and universal recognition, as property in a house, a mine, a farm, or a ship. As a consequence of failure in this respect there prevailed, and most especially throughout the Eastern States, a general impression that there was really but one side to the question; that the cause of the plaintiffs was that of truth; that in the past might had triumphed over right; that, however doubtful might be the expediency of making a decree to that effect, there could be little doubt that justice would thereby be done; and that, while rejecting as wholly inexpedient the idea of perpetuity, there could be but slight objection to so far recognizing that of universality as to grant to British authors the same privileges that thus far had been accorded to our own.

Throughout those years, nevertheless, the effort to obtain from the legislative authority a decree to that effect had proved an utter failure. Time and again had the case been up for trial, but as often had the plaintiffs' counsel wholly failed to agree among themselves as to the consequences that might reasonably be expected to result from recognition of their clients' so-called rights. Northern and Eastern advocates, representing districts in which schools and colleges abounded, insisted that perpetuity and universality of privilege must result in giving the defendants cheaper books. Southern counsel, on the contrary, representing districts in which schools were rare, and students few in number, insisted that extension of privilege would have the effect of giving to planters handsome editions of the works they needed, while preventing the publication of "cheap and nasty" editions, fitted for the "mudsills" of Northern States. Failing thus to agree among themselves they failed to convince the jury, mainly representing, as it did, the Centre and the West, as a consequence of which, verdicts favorable to the defendants had, on each and every occasion, been rendered.

A thoroughly adverse popular will having thus been manifested, it was now determined to try the Senate, and here the chances for privilege were better. With a population little greater than that of Pennsylvania, the New England States had six times the Senatorial representation. With readers not a fifth as numerous as were those of Ohio, Carolina, Florida, and Georgia had thrice the number of Senators. By combining these heterogeneous elements the will of the people—so frequently and decidedly expressed—might, it was thought, be set aside. To that end, the Secretary of State, himself one of the plaintiffs, had negotiated the treaty then before the Senate, of the terms of which the defendants had been kept in utter ignorance, and by means of which the principle of taxation without representation was now to be established.

Such was the state of affairs at the date at which, in compliance with the request of a Pennsylvania Senator, the author of these letters put on paper the ideas he had already expressed to him in conversation. By him and other Senators they were held to be conclusive, so conclusive that the plaintiffs were speedily brought to see that the path of safety, for the present at least, lay in the direction of abandoning the treaty and allowing it to be quietly laid in the grave in which it since has rested. That such should have been their course was, at the time, much regretted by the defendants, as they would have greatly preferred an earnest and thorough discussion of the question before the court. Had opportunity been afforded it would have been discussed by one, at least, of the master minds of the Senate;[1] and so discussed as to have satisfied the whole body of our people, authors and editors, perhaps, excepted, that their cause was that of truth and justice; and that if in the past there had been error it had been that of excess of liberality towards the plaintiffs in the suit.

[Footnote 1: Senator Clayton of Delaware.]

The issue that was then evaded is now again presented, eminent counsel having been employed, and the opening speech having just now been made.[2] Having read it carefully, we find in it, however, nothing beyond a labored effort at reducing the literary profession to a level with those of the grocer and the tallow-chandler. It is an elaborate reproduction of Oliver Twist's cry for "more! more!"—a new edition of the "Beggar's Petition," perusal of which must, as we think, have affected with profound disgust many, if not even most, of the eminent persons therein referred to. In it, we have presented for consideration the sad case of one distinguished writer and admirable man who, by means of his pen alone, had been enabled to pass through a long life of most remarkable enjoyment, although his money receipts had, by reason of the alleged injustice of the consumers of his products, but little exceeded $200,000; that of a lady writer who, by means of a sensational novel of great merit and admirably adapted to the modes of thought of the hour, had been enabled to earn in a single year, the large sum of $40,000, though still deprived of two hundred other thousands she is here said to have fairly earned; of a historian whose labors, after deducting what had been applied to the creation of a most valuable library, had scarcely yielded fifty cents per day; of another who had had but $1000 per month; and, passing rapidly from the sublime to the ridiculous, of a school copy-book maker who had seen his improvements copied, without compensation to himself, for the benefit of English children.

[Footnote 2: See Atlantic Monthly for October.]

These may and perhaps should be regarded as very sad facts; but had not the picture a brighter side, and might it not have been well for the eminent counsel to have presented both? Might he not, for instance, have told his readers that, in addition to the $200,000 above referred to, and wholly as acknowledgment of his literary services, the eminent recipient had for many years enjoyed a diplomatic sinecure of the highest order, by means of which he had been enabled to give his time to the collection of materials for his most important works? Might he not have further told us how other of the distinguished men he had named, as well as many others whose names had not been given, have, in a manner precisely similar, been rewarded for their literary labors? Might he not have said something of the pecuniary and societary successes that had so closely followed the appearance of the novel to whose publication he had attributed so great an influence? Might he not, and with great propriety, have furnished an extract from the books of the "New York Ledger," exhibiting the tens and hundreds of thousands that had been paid for articles which few, if any, would care to read a second time? Might he not have told his readers of the excessive earnings of public lecturers? Might he not, too, have said a word or two of the tricks and contrivances that are being now resorted to by men and women—highly respectable men and women too—for evading, on both sides of the Atlantic, the spirit of the copyright laws while complying with their letter?

Would, however, such a course of proceeding have answered his present purpose? Perhaps not! His business was to pass around the hat, accompanying it with a strong appeal to the charity of the defendants, and this, so far as we can see, is all that thus far has been done.

Might not, however, a similar, and yet stronger, appeal now be made in behalf of other of the public servants? At the close of long lives devoted to the public service, Washington, Hamilton, Clay, Clayton, and many other of our most eminent men have found themselves largely losers, not gainers, by public service. The late Governor Andrew's services were surely worth as much, per hour, as those of the authoress of "Uncle Tom's Cabin," yet did he give five years of his life, and perhaps his life itself, for far less than half of what she had received for the labors of a single one. Deducting the expenses incident to his official life, Mr. Lincoln would have been required to labor for five and twenty years before he could have received as much as was paid to the author of the "Sketch Book." The labors of the historian of Ferdinand and Isabella have been, to himself and his family, ten times more productive than have been those of Mr. Stanton, the great war minister of the age.—Turning now, from civil to military life, we see among ourselves officers who have but recently rendered the largest service, but who are now quite coolly whistled down the wind, to find where they can the means of support for wives and children. Studying the lists of honored dead, we find therein the names of men of high renown whose widows and children are now starving on pensions whose annual amount is less than the monthly receipt of any one of the authors above referred to.

Such being the facts, and, that they are facts cannot be denied, let us now suppose a proposition to be made that, with a view to add one, two, three, or four thousand dollars to the annual income of ex-presidents, and ex-legislators, and half as much to that of the widows and children of distinguished officers, there should be established a general pension system, involving an expenditure of the public moneys, and consequent taxation, to the extent of ten or fifteen millions a year, and then inquire by whom it might be supported. Would any single one of the editors who are now so earnest in their appeals for further grants of privilege venture so to do? Would not the most earnest of them be among the first to visit on such a proposition the most withering denunciations? Judging from what, in the last two years, we have read in various editorial columns, we should say that they would be so. Would, however, any member of either house of Congress venture to commit himself before the world by offering such a proposition? We doubt it very much. Nevertheless it is now coolly proposed to establish a system that would not only tax the present generation as many millions annually, but that would grow in amount at a rate far exceeding the growth of population, doing this in the hope that future essayists might be enabled to count their receipts by half instead of quarter millions, and future novelists to collect abroad and at home the hundreds of thousands that, as we are assured, are theirs of right, and that are now denied them. When we shall have determined to grant to the widows and children of the men who in the last half dozen years have perished in the public service, some slight measure of justice, it may be time to consider that question, but until then it should most certainly be deferred.

The most active and earnest of all the advocates of literary rights was, two years since, if the writer's memory correctly serves him, the most thorough and determined of all our journalists in insisting on the prompt dismissal of thousands and tens of thousands of men who, at their country's call, had abandoned the pursuits and profits of civil life. Did he, however, ever propose that they should be allowed any extra pay on which to live, and by means of which to support their wives and children, in the interval between discharge from military service and re-establishment in their old pursuits? Nothing of the kind is now recollected. Would he now advocate the enactment of a law by means of which the widow and children of a major-general who had fallen on the field should, so far as pay was concerned, be placed on a level with an ordinary police officer? He might, but that he would do so could not with any certainty be affirmed. She and they would, nevertheless, seem to have claims on the consideration of American men and women fully equal to those of the authoress of "Lady Audley's Secret," already, as she is understood to be, in the annual receipt from this country of more than thrice the amount of the widow's pension, in addition to tens of thousands at home.[1]

[Footnote 1: The London correspondent of Scribner and Co.'s "Book Buyer" says that Miss Braddon's first publisher, Mr. Tinsley (who died suddenly last year), called the elegant villa he built for himself at Putney "Audley House," in grateful remembrance of the "Lady" to whose "Secret" he was indebted for fortune; and Miss Braddon herself, through her man of business, has recently purchased a stately mansion of Queen Anne's time, "Litchfield House," at Richmond.]

It is, however, as we are gravely told, but ten per cent. that she asks, and who could or should object to payment of such a pittance? Not many, perhaps, if unaccompanied by monopoly privleges that would multiply the ten by ten and make it an hundred! Alone, the cost to our readers might not now exceed an annual million. Let Congress then pass an act appropriating that sum to be distributed among foreign authors whose works had been, or might be republished here. That should have the writer's vote, but he objects, and will continue to object, to any legislative action that shall tend towards giving to already "great and wealthy" publishing houses the nine millions that they certainly will charge for collecting the single one that is to go abroad.

"Great and wealthy" as they are here said to be, and as they certainly are, we are assured that even they have serious troubles, against which they greatly need to be protected. In common with many heretofore competing railroad companies they have found that, however competition among themselves might benefit the public, it would tend rather to their own injury, and therefore have they, by means of most stringent rules, established a "courtesy" copyright, the effect of which exhibits itself in the fact, that the prices of reprinted books are now rapidly approaching those of domestic production. Further advances in that direction might, however, prove dangerous; "courtesy" rules not, as we are here informed, being readily susceptible of enforcement. A salutary fear of interlopers still restrains those "great and wealthy houses," at heavy annual cost to themselves, and with great saving to consumers of their products. That this may all be changed; that they may build up fortunes with still increased rapidity; that they may, to a still greater extent, monopolize the business of publication; and, that the people may be taxed to that effect; all that is now needed is, that Congress shall pass a very simple law by means of which a few men in Eastern cities shall be enabled to monopolize the business of republication, secure from either Eastern or Western competition. That done, readers will be likely to see a state of things similar to that now exhibited at Chicago, where railroad companies that have secured to themselves all the exits and entrances of the city, are, as we are told, at this moment engaged in organizing a combination that shall have the effect of dividing in fair proportion among the wolves the numerous flocks of sheep.

On all former occasions Northern advocates of literary monopolies assured us that it was in that direction, and in that alone, we were to look for the cheapening of books. Now, nothing of this sort is at all pretended. On the contrary, we are here told of the extreme impropriety of a system which makes it necessary for a New England essayist to accept a single dollar for a volume that under other circumstances would sell for half a guinea; of the wrong to such essayists that results from the issue of cheap "periodicals made up of selections from the reviews and magazines of Europe;" of the "abominable extravagance of buying a great and good novel in a perishable form for a few cents;" of the increased accessibility of books by the "masses of the people" that must result from increasing prices; and of the greatly increased facility with which circulating libraries may be formed whensoever the "great and wealthy houses" shall have been given power to claim from each and every reader of Dickens's novels, as their share of the monopoly profits, thrice as much as he now pays for the book itself! This, however, is only history repeating itself with a little change of place, the argument of to-day, coming from the North, being an almost exact repetition of that which, twenty years since, came from the South—from the mouths of men who rejoiced in the fact that no newspapers were published in their districts, and who well knew that the way towards preventing the dissemination of knowledge lay in the direction of granting the monopoly privileges that had been asked. The anti-slavery men of the present thus repeat the argument of the pro-slavery men of the past, extremes being thus brought close together.

Our people are here assured that Russia, Sweden, and other countries are ready to unite with them in recognizing the "rights" now claimed. So, too, it may be well believed, would it be with China, Japan, Bokhara, and the Sandwich Islands. Of what use, however, would be such an union? Would it increase the facilities for transplanting the ideas of American authors? Are not the obstacles to such transplantation already sufficiently great, and is it desirable that they should be at all increased? Germany has already tried the experiment, but whether or not, when the time shall come, the existing treaties will be renewed, is very doubtful. Where she now pays dollars, she probably receives cents. Discussion of the question there has led to the translation and republication of the letters here now republished, and the views therein expressed have received the public approbation of men whose opinions are entitled to the highest consideration. What has recently been done in that country in reference to domestic copyright, and what has been the effect, are well exhibited in an article from an English journal just now received, a part of which, American moneys having been substituted for German ones, is here given, as follows:

"We have so long enjoyed the advantage of unrestricted competition in the production of the works of the best English writers of the past, that we can hardly realize what our position would have been had the right to produce Shakespeare, or Milton, or Goldsmith, or any of our great classic writers, been monopolized by any one publishing-house,—certainly we should never have seen a shilling Shakespeare, or a half-crown Milton; and Shakespeare, instead of being, as he is,' familiar in our mouths as household words,' would have been known but to the scholar and the student. We are far from condemning an enlightened system of copyright, and have not a word to say in favor of unreasoning competition; but we do think that publishers and authors often lose sight of their own interest in adhering to a system of high prices and restricted sale. Tennyson's works supply us with a case in point—here, to possess a set of Tennyson's poems, a reader must pay something like 38_s_. or 40_s_.—in Boston you may buy a magnificent edition of all his works in two volumes for something like 15_s_., and a small edition for some four or five shillings. The result is the purchasers in England are numbered by hundreds, in America by thousands. In Germany we have almost a parallel case. There the works of the great German poets, of Schiller, of Goethe, of Jean Paul, of Wieland, and of Herder, are at the present time 'under the protecting privileges of the most illustrious German

Confederation,' and, by special privilege, the exclusive property of the Stuttgart publishing firm of J. G. Cotta. On the forthcoming 9th of November this monopoly will cease, and all the works of the above-mentioned poets will be open to the speculation of German publishers generally. It may be interesting to our readers to learn the history of these peculiar legal restrictions, which have so long prevailed in the German booktrade, and the results likely to follow from their removal.

"Until the beginning of this century literary piracy was not prohibited in the German States. As, however, protection of literary productions was, at last, emphatically urged, the Acts of the Confederation (on the reconstruction of Germany in the year 1815) contained a passage to the effect, that the Diet should, at its first meeting, consider the necessity of uniform laws for securing the rights of literary men and publishers. The Diet moved in the matter in the year 1818, appointing a commission to settle this question; and, thanks to that supreme profoundness which was ever applied to the affairs of the father-land by this illustrious body, after twenty-two years of deliberation, on the 9th of Nov., 1837, decreed the law, that the rights of authorship should be acknowledged and respected, at least, for the space of ten years; copyright for a longer period, however, being granted for voluminous and costly works, and for the works of the great German poets.

"In the course of time, however, a copyright for ten years proved insufficient even for the commonest works; it was therefore extended by a decree of the Diet, dated June 19, 1845, over the natural term of the author's life and for thirty years after his death. With respect to the works of all authors deceased before the 9th of November, 1837— including the works of the poets enumerated above—the Diet decided that they could all be protected until the 9th of November, 1867.

"It was to be expected that the firm of J. G. Cotta, favored until now with so valuable a monopoly, would make all possible exertions not to be surpassed in the coming battle of the Publishers, though it is a somewhat curious sight to see this haughty house, after having used its privileges to the last moment, descend now suddenly from its high monopolistic stand into the arena of competition, and compete for public favor with its plebeian rivals. Availing itself of the advantage which the monopoly hitherto attached to it naturally gives it, the house has just commenced issuing a cheap edition of the German classics, under the title 'Bibliothek für Alle. Meisterwerke deutscher Classiker,' in weekly parts, 6 cts. each; containing the selected works of Schiller, at the price of 75 cts., and the selected works of Goethe, at the price of $1.50. And now, just as the monopoly is gliding from their hands, the same firm offers, in a small 16mo edition, Schiller's complete works, 12 vols., for 75 cts.

"Another publisher, A. H. Payne, of Leipzig, announces a complete edition of Schiller's works, including some unpublished pieces, for 75 cts.

"Again, the well-known firm of F. A. Brockhaus holds out a prospectus of a corrected critical edition of the German poets of the eighteenth and nineteenth century, which we have every reason to believe will merit success. A similar enterprise is announced, just now, by the Bibliographical Institution of Hildburghausen, under the title, 'Bibliothek der deutschen Nationalliteratur,' edited by Heinr. Kurz, in weekly parts of 10 sheets, at the price of 12 cts. each. Even an illustrated edition of the Classics will be presented to the public, in consequence of the expiration of the copyright. The Grotesche Buchhandlung, of Berlin, is issuing the 'Hausbibliothek deutscher Classiker,' with wood-cut illustrations by such eminent artists as Richter, Thumann, and others; and the first part, just published, containing Louise, by Voss, with truly artistic illustrations, has met with general approbation. But, above all, the popular edition of the poets, issued by G. Hempel, of Berlin, under the general title of 'National Bibliothek sämmtlicher deutscher Classiker,' 8vo. in parts, 6 cts. each, seems destined to surpass all others in popularity, though not in merit. Of the first part (already published), containing Bürger's Poems, 300,000 copies have been sold, and 150,000 subscribers' names have been registered for the complete series. This immense sale, unequalled in the annals of the German book-trade, will certainly induce many other publishers to embark in similar enterprises."—Trübner's Literary Record, Oct. 1867.

Judging from this, there will, five years hence, be a million of families in possession of the works of Schiller, Bürger, Goethe, Herder and others, that thus far have been compelled to dispense with their perusal. Sad to think, however, they will be of those cheap editions now so much despised by American advocates of monopoly privileges! How much better for the German people would it not have been had their Parliament recognized the perpetuity of literary rights, and thus enabled the "great and wealthy house" of Cotta and Co. to carry into full effect the idea that their own editions should alone be published, thereby adding other millions to the very many of which they already are the owners!

At this moment a letter from Mr. Bayard Taylor advises us that German circulating libraries impede the sale of books; that the circulation of even highly popular works is limited within 20,000; and that, as a necessary consequence, German authors are not paid so well as of right they should be.[1] This, however, is precisely the state of things that, as we are now assured, should be brought about in this country, prices being raised, and readers being driven to the circulating library by reason of the deficiency of the means required for forming the private one. It is the one that would be brought about should our authors, unhappily for themselves, succeed in obtaining what is now demanded.

[Footnote 1: New York Tribune, Nov. 29]

The day has passed, in this country, for the recognition of either perpetuity or universality of literary rights. The wealthy Carolinian, anxious that books might be high in price, and knowing well that monopoly privileges were opposed to freedom, gladly cooperated with Eastern authors and publishers, anti-slavery as they professed to be. The enfranchised black, on the contrary, desires that books may be cheap, and to that end he and his representatives will be found in all the future co-operating with the people of the Centre and the West in maintaining the doctrine that literary privileges exist in virtue of grants from the people who own the materials out of which books are made; that those privileges have been perhaps already too far extended; that there exists not even a shadow of reason for any further extension; and that to grant what now is asked would be a positive wrong to the many millions of consumers, as well as an obstacle to be now placed in the road towards civilization.

The amount now paid for public service under our various governments is more than, were it fairly distributed, would suffice for giving proper reward to all. Unfortunately the distribution is very bad, the largest compensation generally going to those who render the smallest service. So, too, is it with regard to literary employments; and so is it likely to continue throughout the future. Grant all that now is asked, and the effect will be seen in the fact, that of the vastly increased taxation ninety per cent. will go to those who work for money alone, and are already overpaid, leaving but little to be added to the rewards of conscientious men with whom their work is a labor of love, as is the case with the distinguished author of the "History of the Netherlands."

Twenty years ago, Macaulay advised his literary friends to be content, believing, as he told them, that the existing "wholesome copyright" was likely to "share in the disgrace and danger" of the more extended one which they then so much desired to see created. Let our authors reflect on this advice! Success now, were it possible that it should be obtained, would be productive of great danger in the already not distant future. In the natural course of things, most of our authorship, for many years to come, will be found east of the Hudson, most of the buyers of books, meanwhile, being found south and west of that river. International copyright will give to the former limited territory an absolute monopoly of the business of republication, the then great cities of the West being almost as completely deprived of participation therein as are now the towns and cities of Canada and Australia. On the one side, there will be found a few thousand persons interested in maintaining the monopolies that had been granted to authors and publishers, foreign and domestic. On the other, sixty or eighty millions, tired of taxation and determined that books shall be more cheaply furnished. War will then come, and the domestic author, sharing in the "disgrace and danger" attendant upon his alliance with foreign authors and domestic publishers, may perhaps find reason to rejoice if the people fail to arrive at the conclusion that the last extension of his own privileges had been inexpedient and should be at once recalled. Let him then study that well-known fable of Aesop entitled "The Dog and the Shadow," and take warning from it!

The writer of these Letters had no personal interest in the question therein discussed. Himself an author, he has since gladly witnessed the translation and republication of his works in various countries of Europe, his sole reason for writing them having been found in a desire for strengthening the many against the few by whom the former have so long, to a greater or less extent, been enslaved. To that end it is that he now writes, fully believing that the right is on the side of the consumer of books, and not with their producers, whether authors or publishers. Between the two there is, however, a perfect harmony of all real and permanent interests, and greatly will he be rejoiced if he shall have succeeded in persuading even some few of his literary countrymen that such is the fact, and that the path of safety will be found in the direction of letting well enough alone.

The reward of literary service, and the estimation in which literary men are held, both grow with growth in that power of combination which results from diversification of employments; from bringing consumers and producers close together; and from thus stimulating the activity of the societary circulation. Both decline as producers and consumers become more widely separated and as the circulation becomes more languid, as is the case in all the countries now subjected to the British free trade influence. Let American authors then unite in asking of Congress the establishment of a fixed and steady policy which shall have the effect of giving us that industrial independence without which there can be neither political nor literary independence. That once secured, they would thereafter find no need for asking the establishment of a system of taxation which would prove so burdensome to our people as, in the end, to be ruinous to themselves.

H. C. C.

PHILADELPHIA,

Dec. 1867.

LETTERS ON INTERNATIONAL COPYRIGHT

LETTER I.

Dear Sir:—You ask for information calculated to enable you to act understandingly in reference to the international copyright treaty now awaiting the action of the Senate. The subject is an important one, more so, as I think, than is commonly supposed, and being very glad to see that it is now occupying your attention, it will afford me much pleasure to comply, as far as in my power, with your request.

Independently of the principle involved, it seems to me that the course now proposed to be pursued is liable to very grave objection. It is an attempt to substitute the action of the Executive for that of the Legislature, and in a case in which the latter is fully competent to do the work. For almost twenty years, Congress has been besieged with applications on the subject, but without effect. Senate Committees have reported in favor of the measure, but the lower House, composed of the direct representatives of the people, has remained unmoved. In despair of succeeding under any of the ordinary forms of proceeding, its friends have invoked the legislation of the Executive power, and the result is seen in the fact, that the Senate, as a branch of the Executive, is now called upon to sanction a law, in the enactment of which the House of Representatives could not be induced to unite. This may be, and doubtless is, in accordance with the letter of the Constitution, but it is so decidedly in opposition to its spirit that, even were there no other objection, the treaty should be rejected. That, however, is but the smallest of the objections to it.

If the people required such a law, nothing could be more easy than to act in this case as we have done before in similar ones. When we desired to arrange for reciprocity in relation to navigation, we fixed the terms, and declared that all the other nations of the earth might accede to them if they would. No treaty was needed, and we therefore became bound to no one. It was in our power to repeal the law when we chose. So, again, in regard to patents. Foreigners exercise the power of patenting their inventions, but they do so under a law that is liable to repeal at the pleasure of Congress. In both of these cases, the bills underwent public discussion, and the people that were to be subjected to the law, saw, and understood, and amended the bills before they became laws. Contrast, I beg of you, this course of proceeding with the one now proposed to be pursued in reference to one of the largest branches of our internal trade. Finding that no bill that could be prepared could stand the ordeal of public discussion, a treaty has been negotiated, the terms of which seem to be known to none but the negotiators, and that treaty has been sent to your House of Congress, there to be discussed in secret session by a number of gentlemen, most of whom have given little attention to the general principle involved, while not even a single one can be supposed qualified to judge of the practical working of the provisions by whose aid the principle is to be carried out. Once confirmed, the treaty can be changed only with the consent of England. Here we have secrecy in the making of laws, and irrevocability of the law when made; whereas, in all other cases, we have had publicity and revocability. Legislation like that now proposed would seem to be better suited to the monarchies of Europe, than to the republic of the United States. The reason why this extraordinary course has been adopted is, that the people have never required the passage of such a law, and could not be persuaded to sanction it now, were it submitted to them.

The French and English copyright treaty has, as I understand, caused great deterioration in the value of property that had been accumulated in France under the system that had before existed, and such may prove to be the case with the one now under consideration. Should it be so, the deterioration would prove to be fifty times greater in amount than it was in France. Will it do so? No one knows, because those whose interests are to be affected by the law are not permitted to read the law that is to be made. They know well that they have not been consulted, and equally well do they know that the negotiator is not familiar with the trade that is to be regulated, and is liable, therefore, to have given his assent to provisions that will work injury never contemplated by him at the time the treaty had been made. Again, provisions may have been inserted, with a view to prevent injury to the publishers, or to the public, that would be found in practice to be utterly futile, or even to augment the difficulty instead of remedying it. That such result would follow the adoption of some of those whose insertion has been urged, I can positively assert. In this state of things, it would seem to be proper that we should know whether the provisions of the treaty were submitted to the examination of any of the parties interested for or against it, and if so, to whom. So far as I can learn, none of those opposed to it have had any opportunity afforded them of reading the law, and if any advice has been taken, it must have been of those publishers who are in favor of it. Those gentlemen, however, are precisely the persons likely most to profit by the adoption of the principle recognized by the treaty; and the more disadvantageous to others the provisions for carrying that principle into effect, the greater must be the advantage to themselves. They, therefore, can be regarded as little more than the exponents of the wishes of their English friends, who were counselling the British Minister on the one hand, while on the other they were, through their friends here, counselling the American one. A treaty negotiated under such circumstances, would seem little likely to provide for the general interests of the American people.

When, in 1837, the attempt was first made to secure for English authors the privilege of copyright, a large number of them united in an agreement declaring a certain New York house to be "the sole authorized publishers and issuers" of their works. Now, had that house volunteered its advice to the Secretary of State of that day, he would scarcely have regarded it as sufficiently disinterested to be qualified for the office it had undertaken; and yet, if any advice in the present case has been asked, it would seem that it must have been from houses that now look forward to filling the place then occupied by that single one, and that cannot, therefore, be regarded as fitted for the office of counsellors to the Secretary of the present day. Recollect, I am, as is everybody else, entirely in the dark. No one knows who furnished advice as to the treaty, nor does any one know what is to be the law when it shall have been confirmed. Neither can any one tell how the errors that may now be made will be corrected. With a law regularly passed through both Houses of Congress, these difficulties could not arise. They are a natural consequence of this attempt to substitute the will of the Executive for that of the people, as expressed by the House of Representatives, and should, as I think, weigh strongly on the minds of Senators when called to vote upon the treaty. Their constituents have a right to see, and to discuss, the laws that are proposed before those laws are finally made, and whenever it is attempted, as in the present case, to stifle discussion, we may reasonably infer that wrong is about to be done. This is, I believe, the first case in which, on account of the unpopularity of the law proposed, it has been attempted to deprive the popular branch of Congress of its constitutional share in legislation, and if this be sanctioned it is difficult to see what other interests may not be subjected to similar action on the part of the Executive. In all such cases, it is the first step that is most difficult, and before making the one now proposed, you should, as I think, weigh well the importance of the precedent about to be established. No one can hold in greater respect than I do, the honorable gentleman who negotiated this treaty; but in thus attempting to substitute the executive will for legislative action, he seems to me to have made a grave mistake.

In the claim now made in behalf of English authors, there is great apparent justice; but that which is not true, often puts on the appearance of truth. For thousands of years, it seemed so obviously true that the sun revolved around the earth that the fact was not disputed, and yet it came finally to be proved that the earth revolved around the sun. Ricardo's theory of the occupation of the earth, the foundation-stone of his system, had so much apparent truth to recommend it, that it was almost universally adopted, and is now the basis of the whole British politico-economical system; and yet the facts are directly the reverse of what Ricardo had supposed them to be. Such being the case, it might be that, upon a full examination of the subject, we should find that, in admitting the claim of foreign authors, we should be doing injustice and not justice. The English press has, it is true, for many years been engaged in teaching us that we were little better than thieves or pirates; but that press has been so uniformly and unsparingly abusive of us, whenever we have failed to grant all that it has claimed, that its views are entitled to little weight. At home, many of our authors have taken the same side of the question; and the only answer that has ever, to my knowledge, been made, has been, that if we admitted the claims of foreign authors, the prices of books would be raised, and the people would be deprived of their accustomed supplies of cheap literature—as I think, a very weak sort of defense. If nothing better than this can be said, we may as well at once plead guilty to the charge of piracy, and commence a new and more honest course of action. Evil may not be done that good may come of it, nor may we steal an author's brains that our people may be cheaply taught. To admit that the end justifies the means, would be to adopt the line of argument so often used by English speakers, in and out of Parliament, when they defend the poisoning of the Chinese people by means of opium introduced in defiance of their government, because it furnishes revenue to India; or that which teaches that Canada should be retained as a British colony, because of the facility it affords for violation of our laws; or that which would have us regard smugglers, in general, as the great reformers of the age. We stand in need of no such morality as this. We can afford to pay for what we want; but, even were it otherwise, our motto here, and everywhere, should be the old French one: "Fais ce que doy, advienne que pourra"—Act justly, and leave the result to Providence. Before acting, however, we should determine on which side justice lies. Unless I am greatly in error, it is not on the side of international copyright. My reasons for this belief will now be given.

The facts or ideas contained in a book constitute its body. The language in which they are conveyed to the reader constitute the clothing of the body. For the first no copyright is allowed. Humboldt spent many years of his life in collecting facts relative to the southern portion of this continent; yet so soon as he gave them to the light they ceased to be his, and became the common property of all mankind. Captain Wilkes and his companions spent several years in exploring the Southern Ocean, and brought from there a vast amount of new facts, all of which became at once common property. Sir John Franklin made numerous expeditions to the North, during which he collected many facts of high importance, for which he had no copyright. So with Park, Burkhard, and others, who lost their lives in the exploration of Africa. Captain McClure has just accomplished the Northwest Passage, yet has he no exclusive right to the publication of the fact. So has it ever been. For thousands of years men like these— working men, abroad and at home—have been engaged in the collection of facts; and thus there has been accumulated a vast body of them, all of which have become common property, while even the names of most of the men by whom they were collected have passed away. Next to these come the men who have been engaged in the arrangement of facts and in their comparison, with a view to deduce therefrom the laws by which the world is governed, and which constitute science. Copernicus devoted his life to the study of numerous facts, by aid of which he was at length enabled to give to the world a knowledge of the great fact that the earth revolved around the sun; but he had therein, from the moment of its publication, no more property than had the most violent of his opponents., The discovery of other laws occupied the life of Kepler, but he had no property in them. Newton spent many years of his life in the composition of his "Principia," yet in that he had no copyright, except for the mere clothing in which his ideas were placed before the world. The body was common property. So, too, with Bacon and Locke, Leibnitz and Descartes, Franklin, Priestley, and Davy, Quesnay, Turgot, and Adam Smith, Lamarck and Cuvier, and all other men who have aided in carrying science to the point at which it has now arrived. They have had no property in their ideas. If they labored, it was because they had a thirst for knowledge. They could expect no pecuniary reward, nor had they much reason even to hope for fame. New ideas were, necessarily, a subject of controversy; and cases are, even in our time, not uncommon, in which the announcement of an idea at variance with those commonly recorded has tended greatly to the diminution of the enjoyment of life by the man by whom it has been announced. The contemporaries of Harvey could scarcely be made to believe in the circulation of the blood. Mr. Owen might have lived happily in the enjoyment of a large fortune had he not conceived new views of society. These he gave to the world in the form of a book, that led him into controversy which has almost lasted out his life, while the effort to carry his ideas into effect has cost him his fortune. Admit that he had been right, and that the correctness of his views were now fully established, he would have in them no property whatever; nor would his books be now yielding him a shilling, because later writers would be placing them before the world in other and more attractive clothing. So is it with the books of all the men I have named. The copyright of the "Principia" would be worth nothing, as would be the case with all that Franklin wrote on electricity, or Davy on chemistry. Few now read Adam Smith, and still fewer Bacon, Leibnitz, or Descartes. Examine where we may, we shall find that the collectors of the facts and the producers of the ideas which constitute the body of books, have received little or no reward while thus engaged in contributing so largely to the augmentation of the common property of mankind.

For what, then, is copyright given? For the clothing in which the body is produced to the world. Examine Mr. Macaulay's "History of England" and you will find that the body is composed of what is common property. Not only have the facts been recorded by others, but the ideas, too, are derived from the works of men who have labored for the world without receiving, and frequently without the expectation of receiving, any pecuniary compensation for their labors. Mr. Macaulay has read much and carefully, and he has thus been enabled to acquire great skill in arranging and clothing his facts; but the reader of his books will find in them no contribution to positive knowledge. The works of men who make contributions of that kind are necessarily controversial and distasteful to the reader; for which reason they find few readers, and never pay their authors. Turn now to our own authors, Prescott and Bancroft, who have furnished us with historical works of so great excellence, and you will find a state of things precisely similar. They have taken a large quantity of materials out of the common stock, in which you, and I, and all of us have an interest; and those materials they have so reclothed as to render them attractive of purchasers; but this is all they have done. Look to Mr. Webster's works, and you will find it the same. He was a great reader. He studied the Constitution carefully, with a view to understand what were the views of its authors, and those views he reproduced in different and more attractive clothing, and there his work ended. He never pretended, as I think, to furnish the world with any new ideas; and if he had done so, he could have claimed no property in them. Few now read the heavy volumes containing the speeches of Fox and Pitt. They did nothing but reproduce ideas that were common property, and in such clothing as answered the purposes of the moment. Sir Robert Peel did the same. The world would now be just as wise had he never lived, for he made no contribution to the general stock of knowledge. The great work of Chancellor Kent is, to use the words of Judge Story, "but a new combination and arrangement of old materials, in which the skill and judgment of the author in the selection and exposition, and accurate use of those materials, constitute the basis of his reputation, as well as of his copyright." The world at large is the owner of all the facts that have been collected, and of all the ideas that have been deduced from them, and its right in them is precisely the same that the planter has in the bale of cotton that has been raised on his plantation; and the course of proceeding of both has, thus far, been precisely similar; whence I am induced to infer that, in both cases, right has been done. When the planter hands his cotton to the spinner and the weaver, he does not say, "Take this and convert it into cloth, and keep the cloth;" but he does say, "Spin and weave this cotton, and for so doing you shall have such interest in the cloth as will give you a fair compensation for your labor and skill, but, when that shall have been paid, the cloth will be mine." This latter is precisely what society, the owner of facts and ideas, says to the author: "Take these raw materials that have been collected, put them together, and clothe them after your own fashion, and for a given time we will agree that nobody else shall present them in the same dress. During that time you may exhibit them for your own profit, but at the end of that period the clothing will become common property, as the body now is. It is to the contributions of your predecessors to our common stock that you are indebted for the power to make your book, and we require you, in your turn, to contribute towards the augmentation of the stock that is to be used by your successors." This is justice, and to grant more than this would be injustice.

Let us turn now, for a moment, to the producers of works of fiction. Sir Walter Scott had carefully studied Scottish and Border history, and thus had filled his mind with facts preserved, and ideas produced, by others, which he reproduced in a different form. He made no contribution to knowledge. So, too, with our own very successful Washington Irving. He drew largely upon the common stock of ideas, and dressed them up in a new, and what has proved to be a most attractive form. So, again, with Mr. Dickens. Read his "Bleak House" and you will find that he has been a most careful observer of men and things, and has thereby been enabled to collect a great number of facts that he has dressed up in different forms, but that is all he has done. He is in the condition of a man who had entered a large garden and collected a variety of the most beautiful flowers growing therein, of which he had made a fine bouquet. The owner of the garden would naturally say to him: "The flowers are mine, but the arrangement is yours. You cannot keep the bouquet, but you may smell it, or show it for your own profit, for an hour or two, but then it must come to me. If you prefer it, I am willing to pay you for your services, giving you a fair compensation for your time and taste." This is exactly what society says to Mr. Dickens, who makes such beautiful literary bouquets. What is right in the individual, cannot be wrong in the mass of individuals of which society is composed. Nevertheless, the author objects to this, insisting that he is owner of the bouquet itself, although he has paid no wages to the man who raised the flowers. Were he asked to do so, he would, as I shall show in another letter, regard it as leading to great injustice.

LETTER II.

Let us suppose, now, that you should move, in the Senate, a resolution looking to the establishment of the exclusive right of making known the facts, or ideas, that might be brought to light, and see what would be the effect. You would, as I think, find yourself at once surrounded by the gentlemen who dress up those facts and ideas, and issue them in the form of books. The geographer would say to you: "My dear sir, this will never do. Look at my book, and you will see that it is drawn altogether from the works of others, many of whom have sunk their fortunes, while others have lost their lives, in pursuit of the knowledge that I so cheaply give the world. You will find there the essence of the works of Humboldt, and of Wilkes. All of Franklin's discoveries are there, and I am now waiting only for the appearance of McClure's voyage in the Arctic regions to give a new edition of my book. Reflect, I beseech you, upon what you are about to do. Very few persons have leisure to read, or means to pay for the books of these travellers. A few hundred copies are sufficient to satisfy the demand, and then their works die out. Of mine, on the contrary, the sale is ten, fifteen, or twenty thousand annually, and thus is knowledge disseminated throughout the world, enabling the men who furnish me with facts to reap a rich harvest of never dying fame. Grant them a copyright to the new ideas they may supply to the world, and at once you put a stop to the production of such books as mine, to my great injury and to the loss of mankind at large. Facts and ideas are common property, and their owners, the public, have a right to use them as they will."

The historian would say: "Mr. Senator, if you persist in this course, you will never again see histories like mine. Here are hundreds of people scattered over the country, industriously engaged in disinterring facts relating to our early history. They are enthusiasts, and many of them are very poor. Some of them contrive to publish, in the form of books, the results of their researches, while others give them to the newspapers, or to the historical societies, and thus they are enabled to come before the world. Few people buy such things, and it not unfrequently happens that men who have spent their lives in the collection of important facts, waste much of their small means in giving them to an ungrateful nation. Nevertheless, they have their reward in the consciousness that they are thus enabling others to furnish the world with accurate histories of their country. I find them of infinite use. They are my hewers of wood and drawers of water, and they never look for payment for their labor. Deprive me of their services, and I shall be obliged to abandon the production of books, and return to the labors of my profession—and they will be deprived of fame, while the public will be deprived of knowledge."

The medical writer would say: "Mr. Senator, should you succeed in carrying out the idea with which you have commenced, you will, I fear, be the cause of great injury to our profession, and probably of great loss of life, for you will thereby arrest the dissemination of knowledge. We have, here and abroad, thousands of industrious and thoughtful men, more intent upon doing good than upon pecuniary profit, who give themselves to the study of particular diseases, furnishing the results to our journals, and not unfrequently publishing monographs of the highest value. The sale of these is always small, and their publication not unfrequently makes heavy drafts on the small means of their authors. Such men are of infinite use to me, for it is by aid of their most valuable labors that I have found myself enabled to prepare the numerous and popular works that I have given to the world. Look at them. There are several volumes of each, of which I sell thousands annually, to my great profit. Deprive me of the power to avail myself of the brains of the working men of the profession and my books will soon cease to be of any value, and I shall lose the large income now realized from them, while the public will suffer in their health by reason of the increased difficulty of disseminating information."

The professor would ask you to look at his lectures and satisfy yourself that they contained no single idea that had originated with himself. "How," he would ask, "could these valuable lectures have been produced, had I been deprived of the power to avail myself of the facts collected by the working-men, and the principles deduced from them by the thinkers of the world? I have no leisure to collect facts or analyze them. For many years past, these lectures have yielded me a large income, and so will they continue to do, provided I be allowed to do in future as in time past I have done, appropriate to my own use all the new facts and new ideas I meet with, crediting their authors or not as I find it best to suit my purpose. Abandon your idea, my dear sir; it cannot be carried out. The men who work, and the men who think, must content themselves with fame, and be thankful if the men who write books and deliver lectures do not appropriate to themselves the entire credit of the facts they use, and the ideas they borrow."

The teacher of natural science would say: "My friend, have you reflected on what you are about to do? Look at our collections, and see how they have been enlarged within the last half century. Asia and Africa, and the islands of the Southern Ocean, have been traversed by indefatigable men who, at the hazard of life, and often at the cost of fortune, have quadrupled our knowledge of vegetable and animal life. Such men do not ask for compensation of any kind. They are willing to work for nothing. Why, then, not let them? Look at the vast contributions to geological knowledge that have been made throughout the Union by men who were content with a bare support, and glad to have the results of their labors published, as they have been, at the public cost. Such men ask no copyright. When they publish, it is almost always at a loss. Wilson lived and died poor. So did

Audubon, to whose labors we are indebted for so much ornithological knowledge. Morton expended a large sum in the preparation and publication of his work on crania. Agassiz did the same with his great work on fishes. Cuvier had nothing but fame to bequeath to his family. Lamarck's great work on the invertebratae sold so slowly that very many years elapsed before the edition was exhausted; but he would have found his reward had he lived to see his ideas appropriated without acknowledgment, and reclothed by the author of 'Vestiges of Creation,' of which the sale has been so large. This, my friend, is the use for which such men as Lamarck and Cuvier were intended. They collect and classify the facts, and we popularize them to our own profit. Look at my works and see, bulky as they are, how many editions have been printed, and think how profitable they must have been to the publisher and myself. Look further, and see how numerous are the books to which my labors have indirectly given birth. See the many school-books in relation to botany and other departments of natural science, the authors of which know little of what they undertake to teach, except what they have drawn from me and others like myself. Again, see how numerous are the 'Flora's Emblems,' and the 'Garlands of Flowers,' and the 'Flora's Dictionaries,' and how large is their sale— and how large must be the profits of those engaged in their production. To recognize in such men as Cuvier and Lamarck the existence of any right to either their facts or their deductions would be an act of great injustice towards the race of literary men, while most inexpedient as regards the world at large, now so cheaply supplied with knowledge. As regards the question of international copyright now before the Senate, my views are different. Several of my books have been published abroad, and my publisher here tells me, that to prevent the republication of others he is obliged to supply them cheaply for foreign markets, and thus am I deprived of a fair and just reward for my labors. Copyright should be universal and eternal, and such, I am persuaded, will be the result at which you will arrive when you shall have thoroughly studied the subject."

Having studied it, and having given full consideration to the views that they and others had presented, your answer would probably be to the following effect: "It is clear, gentlemen, from your own showing, that there are two distinct classes of persons engaged in the production of books—the men who furnish the body, and those who dress it up for production before the world. The first class are generally poor, and likely to continue so. They labor without any view to pecuniary advantage. They are, too, very generally helpless. Animated to their work solely by a desire to penetrate into the secrets of nature the character of their minds unfits them for mixing in a money-getting world, while you are always in that world, ready to enforce your claims to its consideration. As a consequence of this, they are rarely allowed even the credit that is due to them. Their discoveries become at once common property, to be used by men like yourselves, and for your own individual profit. We have here among ourselves a gentleman who has given to astronomy a new and highly important law essential to the perfection of the science, the discovery of which has cost him the labor of a life, as a consequence of which he is poor and likely so to remain. Important as was his discovery, his name is already so completely forgotten that there is probably not a single one among you that can now recall it, and yet his law figures in all the recent books. Is this right? Has he no claim to consideration?"

"In answer, you will say, that 'to admit the existence of any such rights is not only impossible, but inexpedient, even were it possible. Knowledge advances by slow and almost imperceptible steps, and each is but the precursor of a new and more important one. Were each discoverer of a new truth to be authorized to monopolize the teaching of it millions of men, to whom, by our aid, it is communicated, would remain in ignorance of it, and thus would farther advance be prevented. In all times past, such truths have been regarded as common property; and so,' you will add, 'they must continue to be regarded. Rely upon it, the best interests of society require that such shall continue to be the case, however great the apparent injustice to the discoverer.'

"Here, you will observe, you waive altogether the question of right which you so strongly enforce in regard to yourselves. It may be that you have reason; but if so, how do you yourselves stand in your relations with the great mass of human beings whose right to this common property is equal with your own? For thousands of years working men, collectors of facts and philosophers, have been contributing to the common stock, and the treasure accumulated is now enormously great; and yet the mass of mankind remain still ignorant, and are poor, depraved, and wretched, because ignorant. Under such circumstances, justice would seem to require of the legislator that he should sanction no measure tending to throw unnecessary difficulty in the way of the dissemination of knowledge. To do so, would be to deprive the many of the power to profit by their interest in the common property. To do so, would be to deprive the men who have contributed to the accumulation of this treasure of even the reward to which, as you admit, they justly may make a claim. If they are to be satisfied with fame, we must do nothing tending to limit the dissemination of their ideas, because to do so would be to limit their power to acquire fame. If they are to be satisfied with the idea of doing good to their fellow-men, we must avoid every thing tending to limit the knowledge of their discoveries, because to do so would be to deprive them of much of their small reward. The state of the matter is, as I conceive, as follows: On one side of you stand the contributors to the vast treasure of knowledge that mankind has accumulated, and is accumulating—men who have, in general, labored without fee or reward; on the other side of you stand the owners of this vast treasure, desirous to have it fashioned in a manner to suit their various tastes and powers, that all may be enabled to profit by its possession. Between them stand yourselves, middlemen between the producers and the consumers. It is your province to combine the facts and ideas, as does the manufacturer when he takes the raw materials of cloth, and, by the aid of the skill of numerous working men, past and present, elaborates them into the beautiful forms that so much gratify our eyes in passing through the Crystal Palace. For this service you are to be paid; but to enable you to receive payment you need the aid of the legislator, as the common law grants no more copyright for the form in which ideas are expressed than for the ideas themselves. In granting this aid he is required to see that, while he secures that you have justice, he does no injustice to the men who produce the raw material of your books, nor to the community whose common property it is. In granting it, he is bound to use his efforts to attain the knowledge needed for enabling him to do justice to all parties, and not to you alone. The laws which elsewhere govern the distribution of the proceeds of labor, must apply in your case with equal force. Looking at them, we see that, with the growth of population and of wealth, there is everywhere a tendency to diminution in the proportion of the product that is allowed to the men who stand between the producer and the consumer. In new settlements, trade is small and the shopkeeper requires large profits to enable him to live; and, while the consumer pays a high price, the producer is compelled to be content with a low one. In new settlements, the miller takes a large toll for the conversion of corn into flour, and the spinner and weaver take a large portion of the wool as their reward for converting the balance into cloth. Nevertheless, the shopkeeper, the miller, the spinner, and the weaver are poor, because trade is small. As wealth and population grow, we find the shopkeeper gradually reducing his charge, until from fifty it falls to five per cent.; the miller reducing his, until he finds that he can afford to give all the flour that is yielded by the corn, retaining for himself the bran alone; and the spinner and weaver contenting himself with a constantly diminishing proportion of the wool; and now it is that we find shopkeepers, millers, and manufacturers grow rich, while consumers are cheaply supplied because of the vast increase of trade. In your case, however, the course of proceeding has been altogether different. Half a century since, when our people were but four millions in number, and were poor and scattered, gentlemen like you were secured in the monopoly of their works for fourteen years, with a power of renewal for a similar term. Twenty years since, when the population had almost tripled, and their wealth had sixfold increased, and when the facilities of distribution had vastly grown, the term was fixed at twenty-eight years, with renewal to widow or children for fourteen years more. At the present moment, you are secured in a monopoly for forty-two years, among a population of twenty-six millions of people, certain, at the close of twenty years more, to be fifty millions and likely, at the close of another half century, to be a hundred millions, and with facilities, for the disposal of your products, growing at a rate unequaled in the world. With this vast increase of market, and increase of power over that market, the consumer should be supplied more cheaply than in former times; yet such is not the case. The novels of Mrs. Rowson and Charles B. Brown, and the historical works of Dr. Ramsay, persons who then stood in the first rank of authors, sold as cheaply as do now the works of Fanny Fern, the 'Reveries' of Ik Marvel, or the history of Mr. Bancroft; and yet, in the period that has since elapsed, the cost of publication has fallen probably twenty-five per cent. We have here an inversion of the usual order of things, and it is with these facts before us that you claim to have your monopoly extended over another thirty millions of people; in consideration of which, our people are to grant to the authors of foreign countries a monopoly of the privilege of supplying them with books produced abroad. This application strikes me as unwise. It tends to produce inquiry, and that will, probably, in its turn, lead rather to a reduction than an extension of your privileges. Can it be supposed that when, but a few years hence, our population shall have attained a height of fifty millions, with a demand for books probably ten times greater than at present, the community will be willing to continue to you a monopoly, during forty-two years, of the right of presenting a body that is common property, as compensation for putting it in a new suit of clothing? I doubt it much, and would advise you, for your own good, to be content with what you have. Aesop tells us that the dog lost his piece of meat in the attempt to seize a shadow, and such may prove to be the case on this occasion. So, too, may it be with the owners of patents. The discoverers of principles receive nothing, but those who apply them enjoy a monopoly created by law for their use. Everybody uses chloroform, but nobody pays its discoverer. The man who taught us how to convert India rubber into clothing has not been allowed even fame, while our courts are incessantly occupied with the men who make the clothing. Patentees and producers of books are incessantly pressing upon Congress with claims for enlargement of their privileges, and are thus producing the effect of inducing an inquiry into the validity of their claim to what they now enjoy. Be content, my friends; do not risk the loss of a part of what you have in the effort to obtain more."

The question is often asked: Why should a man not have the same claim to the perpetual enjoyment of his book that his neighbor has in regard to the house he has built? The answer is, that the rights of the parties are entirely different. The man who builds a house quarries the stone and makes the bricks of which it is composed, or he pays another for doing it for him.

When finished, his house is all, materials and workmanship, his own. The man who makes a book uses the common property of mankind, and all he furnishes is the workmanship. Society permits him to use its property, but it is on condition that, after a certain time, the whole shall become part of the common stock. To find a parallel case, let it be supposed that liberal men should, out of their earnings, place at the disposal of the people of your town stone, bricks, and lumber, in quantity sufficient to find accommodation for hundreds of people that were unable to provide for themselves; next suppose that in this state of things your authorities should say to any man or men, "Take these materials, and procure lime in quantity sufficient to build a house; employ carpenters, bricklayers, and architects, and then, in consideration of having found the lime and the workmanship, you shall have a right to charge your own price to every person who may, for all times, desire to occupy a room in it "; would this be doing justice to the men who had given the raw materials for public use? Would it be doing justice to the community by which they had been given? Would it not, on the contrary, be the height of injustice? Unquestionably it would, and it would raise a storm that would speedily displace the men who had thus abused their trust. Their successors would then say: "Messrs.—— our predecessors, did what they had no right to do. These materials are common property. They were given without fee or reward, with a view to benefit the whole people of our town, many of whom are badly accommodated, while others are heavily taxed for helping those who are unable to help themselves. To carry out the views of the benevolent men to whom we are indebted for all these stone, bricks, and lumber, they must remain common property. You may, if you will, convert them into a house, and, in consideration of the labor and skill required for so doing, we will grant you, during a certain time, the privilege of letting the rooms, at your own price, to those who desire to occupy them; but at the close of that time the building must become common property, to be disposed of as we please." This is exactly what the community says to the gentlemen who employ themselves in converting its common property into books, and to say more would be doing great injustice.

The length of time for which the building should be thus granted would depend upon the number of persons that would be likely to use the rooms, and the prices they would be willing to pay. If lodgers were likely to be few and poor, a long time would be required to be given; but if, on the contrary, the community were so great and prosperous as to render it certain that all the rooms would be occupied every day in the year, and at such prices as would speedily repay the labor and skill that had been required, the time allowed would be short. Here, as we see, the course of things would be entirely different from that which is observed in regard to books, the monopoly of which has increased in length with the growth, in wealth and number, of the consumers, and is now attempted, by the aid of international copyright, to be extended over millions of men who are yet exempt from its operation.

The people of this country own a vast quantity of wild land, which by slow degrees acquires a money value, that value being due to the contributions of thousands and tens of thousands of people who are constantly making roads towards them, and thus facilitating the exchange of such commodities as may be raised from them. These lands are common property, but the whole body of their owners has agreed that whenever any one of their number desires to purchase out the interest of his partners he may do so at $1.25 per acre. They do not give him any of the common property; they require him to purchase and pay for it.

With authors they pursue a more liberal course. They say: "We have extensive fields in which hundreds of thousands of men have labored for many centuries. They were at first wild lands, as wild as those of the neighborhood of the Rocky Mountains, but this vast body of laborers has felled the trees and drained the swamps, and has thus removed nearly all the difficulties that stood opposed to profitable cultivation. They have also' opened mines of incalculable richness; mines of gold, silver, lead, copper, iron, and other metals, and all of these are common property. The men who executed these important works were our slaves, ill fed, worse clothed, and still worse lodged; and thousands of the most laborious and useful of them have perished of disease and starvation. Great as are the improvements already made, their number is constantly increasing, for we continue to employ such slaves—active, intelligent, and useful men— in extending them, and scarcely a day elapses that does not bring to light some new discovery, tending greatly to increase the value of our common property. We invite you, gentlemen, to come and cultivate these lands and work these mines. They are free to all. During the long period of forty-two years you shall have the whole product of your labor, and all we shall ask of you, at the close of that period, will be that you leave behind the common property of which we are now possessed, increased by the addition of such machinery as you may yourselves have made. The corn that you may have extracted, and the gold and silver that you may have mined during that long period, will be the property of yourselves, your wives, and your children. We charge no rent for the use of the lands, no wages for the labor of our slaves." Not satisfied with this, however, the persons who work these rich fields and mines claim to be absolute owners, not only of all the gold and silver they extract, but of all the machinery they construct out of the common property; and out of this claim grows the treaty now before the Senate.

If justice requires the admission of foreigners to the enjoyment of a monopoly of the sale of their books it should be conceded at once to all, and it should be declared that no book should be printed here without the consent of its author, let him be Englishman, Frenchman, German, Russian, or Hindoo. This would certainly greatly increase the difficulty now existing in relation to the dissemination of knowledge; but if justice does require it let it be done. Would it, however, benefit the men who have real claims on our consideration? Let us see. A German devotes his life to the study of the history of his country, and at length produces a work of great value, but of proportional size. Real justice says that his work may not be used without his permission; that the facts he has brought to light from among the vast masses of original documents he has examined are his property, and can be published by none others but himself. The legislation, whose aid is invoked in the name of justice by literary men, speaks, however, very differently. It says: "This work is very cumbrous. To establish his views this man has gone into great detail. If translated, his book will scarcely sell to such extent as to pay the labor. The facts are common property. Out of this book you can make one that will be much more readable, and that will sell, for it will not be of more than one third the size. Take it, then, and extract all you need, and you will do well. You will have, too, another advantage. Translation confers no reputation; but an original work, such as I now recommend to you, will give you such a standing as may lead you on to fortune. Few people know any thing of the original work, and it will not be necessary for you to mention that all your materials are thence derived." On the other hand, a lady who has read the work of this poor German finds in it an episode that she expands into a novel, which sells rapidly, and she reaps at home a large reward for her labors; while the man who gave her the idea starves in a garret. A literary friend of the lady novelist, delighted with her success, finds in his countrywoman's treasury of facts the material for a poem out of which he, too, reaps a harvest. Both of these are protected by international copyright, because they have furnished nothing but the clothing of ideas; but the man who supplied them with the ideas finds that his book is condensed abroad, and given to the public, perhaps, without even the mention of his name.

The whole tendency of the existing system is to give the largest reward to those whose labors are lightest, and the smallest to those whose labors are most severe; and every extension of it must necessarily look in that direction. The "Mysteries of Paris" were a fortune to Eugene Sue, and "Uncle Tom's Cabin" has been one to Mrs. Stowe. Byron had 2,000 guineas for a volume of "Childe Harold," and Moore 3,000 for his "Lalla Rookh;" and yet a single year should have more than sufficed for the production of any one of them. Under a system of international copyright, Dumas, already so largely paid, would be protected, whereas Thierry, who sacrificed his sight to the gratification of his thirst for knowledge, would not. Humboldt, the philosopher par excellence of the age, would not, because he furnishes his readers with things, and not with words alone. Of the books that record his observations on this continent, but a part has, I believe, been translated into English, and of these but a small portion has been republished in this country, although to be had without claim for copyright. In England their sale has been small, and can have done little more than pay the cost of translation and publication. Had it been required to pay for the privilege of translation, but a small part of even those which have been republished would probably have ever seen the light in any but the language of the author. This great man inherited a handsome property which he devoted to the advancement of science, and what has been his pecuniary reward may be seen in the following statement, derived from an address recently delivered in New York:—

"There are now living in Europe two very distinguished men, barons, both very eminent in their line, both known to the whole civilized world; one is Baron Rothschild, and the other Baron Humboldt; one distinguished for the accumulation of wealth, the other for the accumulation of knowledge. What are the possessions of the philosopher? Why, sir, I heard a gentleman whom I have seen here this afternoon, say that, on a recent visit to Europe, he paid his respects to that distinguished philosopher, and was admitted to an audience. He found him, at the age of 84 years, fresh and vigorous, in a small room, nicely sanded, with a large deal table uncovered in the midst of that room, containing his books and writing apparatus. Adjoining this, was a small bed-room, in which he slept. Here this eminent philosopher received a visitor from the United States. He conversed with him; he spoke of his works. 'My works,' said he, 'you will find in the adjoining library, but I am too poor to own a copy of them. I have not the means to buy a full copy of my own works.'"

After having furnished to the gentlemen who produce books more of the material of which books are composed than has ever been furnished by any other man, this illustrious man finds himself, at the close of life, altogether dependent on the bounty of the Prussian government, which allows him, as I have heard, less than five hundred dollars a year. In what manner, now, would Humboldt be benefited by international copyright? I know of none; but it is very plain to see that Dumas, Victor Hugo, and George Sand, might derive from it immense revenues. In confirmation of this view, I here ask you to review the names of the persons who urge most anxiously the change of system that is now proposed, and see if you can find in it the name of a single man who has done any thing to extend the domain of knowledge. I think you will not. Next look and see if you do not find in it the names of those who furnish the world with new forms of old ideas, and are largely paid for so doing. The most active advocate of international copyright is Mr. Dickens, who is said to realize $70,000 per annum from the sale of works whose composition is little more than amusement for his leisure hours. In this country, the only attempt that has yet been made to restrict the right of translation is in a suit now before the courts, for compensation for the privilege of converting into German a work that has yielded the largest compensation that the world has yet known for the same quantity of literary labor.

We are constantly told that regard to the interests of science requires that we should protect and enlarge the rights of authors; but does science make any such claim for herself? I doubt it. Men who make additions to science know well that they have, and can have, no rights whatever. Cuvier died very poor, and all the copyright that could have been given to him or Humboldt would not have enriched either the one or the other. Laplace knew well that his great work could yield him nothing. Our own Bowditch translated it as a labor of love, and left by his will the means required for its publication. The gentlemen who advocate the interests of science are literary men who use the facts and ideas furnished by scientific men, paying nothing for their use. Now, literature is a most honorable profession, and the gentlemen engaged in it are entitled not only to the respect and consideration of their fellow-men, but also to the protection of the law; but in granting it, the legislator is bound to recollect, that justice to the men who furnish the raw materials of books, and justice to the community that owns those raw materials, require that protection shall not, either in point of space or time, be greater than is required for giving the producer of books a full and fair compensation for his labor. How the present system operates in regard to English and American authors, I propose to consider in another letter.

LETTER III.

We are assured that justice requires the admission of foreign authors to the privilege of copyright, and in support of the claim that she presents are frequently informed of the extreme poverty of many highly popular English writers. Mrs. Inchbald, so well known as author of the "Simple Story" and other novels, as well as in her capacity of editor, dragged on, as we are told, to the age of sixty, a miserable existence, living always in mean lodgings, and suffering frequently from want of the common comforts of life. Lady Morgan, so well known as Miss Owenson, a brilliant and accomplished woman, is now to some extent dependent upon the public charity, administered in the form of a pension of less than five hundred dollars a year. Mrs. Hemans, the universally admired poetess, lived and died in poverty. Laman Blanchard lost his senses and committed suicide in consequence of being compelled, by his extreme poverty, to the effort of writing an article for a periodical while his wife lay a corpse in the house. Miss Mitford, so well known to all of us, found herself, after a life of close economy, so greatly reduced as to have been under the necessity of applying to her American readers for means to extricate her little property from the rude hands of the sheriff. Like Lady Morgan, she is now a public pensioner. Leigh Hunt is likewise dependent on the public charity. Tom Hood, so well known by his "Song of a Shirt"—the delight of his readers, and a mine of wealth to his publishers; a man without vices, and of untiring industry—lived always from day to day on the produce of his labor. On his death-bed, when his lungs were so worn with consumption that he could breathe only through a silver tube, he was obliged to be propped up with pillows, and, with shaking hand and dizzy head, force himself to the task of amusing his readers, that he might thereby obtain bread for his unhappy wife and children. With all his reputation, Moore found it difficult to support his family, and all the comfort of his declining years was due to the charity of his friend, Lord Lansdowne. In one of his letters from Germany, Campbell expresses himself transported with joy at hearing that a double edition of his poems had just been published in London. "This unexpected fifty pounds," says he, "saves me from jail." Haynes Bayley died in extreme poverty. Similar statements are furnished us in relation to numerous others who have, by the use of their pens, largely contributed to the enjoyment and instruction of the people of Great Britain. It would, indeed, be difficult to find very many cases in which it had been otherwise with persons exclusively dependent on the produce of literary labor. With few and brilliant exceptions, their condition appears to have been, and to be, one of almost hopeless poverty. Scarcely any thing short of this, indeed, would induce the acceptance of the public charity that is occasionally doled out in the form of pensions on the literary fund.

This is certainly an extraordinary state of things, and one that makes to our charitable feelings an appeal that is almost irresistible. Nevertheless, before giving way to such feelings, it would be proper to examine into the real cause of all this poverty, with a view to satisfy ourselves if real charity would carry us in the direction now proposed. The skilful physician always studies the cause of disease before he determines on the remedy, and this course is quite as necessary in prescribing for moral as for physical disorder. Failing to do this, we might increase instead of diminishing the evil, and might find at last that we had been taxing ourselves in vain.

What is claimed by English authors is perpetuity and universality of property in the clothing they supply for the body that is furnished to the world by other and unpaid men; and an examination of the course of proceeding in that country for the last century and a half shows that each step that has been taken has been in that direction. While denying to the producers of facts and ideas any right whatsoever, every act of legislation has tended to give more and more control over their dissemination to men who appropriated them to their own use, and brought them in an attractive form before the reader. Early in the last century was passed an act well known as the Statute of Queen Anne, giving to authors fourteen years as the period during which they were to have a monopoly of the peculiar form of words they chose to adopt in coming before the world. The number of persons then living in England and Wales, and subjected to that monopoly, was about five millions. Since that time the field of its operation has been enlarged, until it now embraces not only England and Wales, but Scotland, Ireland, and the British colonies, containing probably thirty-two millions of people who use the English language. The time, too, has been gradually extended until it now reaches forty-two years, or thrice the period for which it was originally granted. Nevertheless, no life is more precarious than that of an Englishman dependent upon literary pursuits for support. Such men are almost universally poor, and leading men among them, Tennyson and Sir Francis Head for instance, gladly accept the public charity, in the form of pensions for less than five hundred dollars a year. This is not a consequence of limitation in the field of action, for that is six times greater than it was when Gay netted £1,600 from a single opera, and Pope received £6,000 for his "Homer;" five times greater than when Fielding had £1,000 for his "Amelia;" and four times more than when Robertson had £4,500 for his "Charles V.," Gibbon £5,000 for the second part of his history, and McPherson £1,200 for his "Ossian."[1] Since that time money has become greatly more abundant and less valuable; and if we desired to compare the reward of these authors with those of the present day, the former should be trebled in amount, which would give Robertson more than sixty thousand dollars for a work that is comprised in three 8vo. volumes of very moderate size. It is not a consequence of limitation of time, for that has grown from fourteen to forty-two years—more than is required for any book except, perhaps, one in five or ten thousand. It should not be a consequence of poverty in the nation, for British writers assure us that wealth so much abounds that wars are needed to prevent its too rapid growth, and that foreign loans are indispensable for enabling the people of Britain to find an outlet for all their vast accumulations. What, then, is the cause of disease? Why is it that in so wealthy a nation literary men and women are so generally poor that it should be required to bring their poverty before the world, to aid in the demand for an extension to other countries of the monopoly so well secured at home? In that country the fortunes of wealthy men count by millions, and, that being the case, an average contribution of a shilling a head towards paying for the copyright of books, would seem to be the merest trifle to be given in return for the pleasure and the instruction derived from the perusal of the works of English authors, and yet even that small sum does not appear to be paid. Thirty-two millions of shillings make almost eight millions of dollars; a sum sufficient to give to six hundred authors more than thirteen thousand dollars a year, being more than half the salary of the chief magistrate of our Union. Admitting, however, that there were a thousand authors worthy to be paid, and that would most certainly cover them all, it would give to each eight thousand dollars, or one third more than we have been accustomed to allow to men who have devoted their lives to the service of the public, and have at length risen to be Secretaries of State. If English authors were thus largely paid, it would be deemed an absurdity to ask an enlargement of their monopoly; but, as they are not thus paid, it is asked. There is probably but a single literary man in England that receives $8,000 a year for his labors, and it may be doubted if it would be possible to name ten whose annual receipts equal $6,000; while those of a vast majority of them are under $1,500, and very many of them greatly under it. Even were we to increase the number of authors to fifteen hundred, one to every 4,000 males between the ages of 20 and 60 in the kingdom, and to allow them, on an average, $2,000 per annum, it would require but three millions of dollars to pay them, and that could be done by an average contribution of five pence per head of the population, a wonderfully small amount to be paid for literary labor by a nation claiming to be the wealthiest in the world. A shilling a head would give to the whole fifteen hundred salaries nearly equal to those of our Secretaries; and yet we see clever and industrious men, writers of eminence whose readers are to be found in every part of the civilized world, living on in hopeless poverty, and dying with the knowledge that they are leaving widows and children to the "tender mercies" of a world in which they themselves have shone and starved. Viewing all these facts, it may, I think, well be doubted if the annual contributions of the people subject to the British copyright act for the support of the persons who produce their books, much exceeds three pence, or six cents, per head; and here it is that we are to find the real difficulty—one not to be removed by us. The home market is the important one, whether for words or things, and when that is bad but little benefit can be derived from any foreign one; and every effort to extend the latter will, under such circumstances, be found to result in disappointment. It can act only as a plaster to conceal the sore, while the sore itself becomes larger and more dangerous from day to day. To effect a cure, the sore itself must be examined and its cause removed. To cure the disease so prevalent among British authors we must first seek for the causes why the home market for the products of their labor is so very small, and that will be found in the steadily growing tendency towards centralization, so obvious in every part of the operations of the British empire. Centralization and civilization have in all countries, and at all periods of the world, been opposed to each other, and that such is here the case can, I think, readily be shown.

[Footnote 1: The several figures here given are from a statement in a British journal. Whether they are perfectly accurate, or not, I have no means of determining.]

Among the earliest cases in which this tendency was exhibited was that of the Union by which the kingdom of Scotland was reduced to the condition of a province of England, and Edinburgh, from being the capital of a nation, to becoming a mere provincial town. By many and enlightened Scotchmen a federal union would have been preferred; but a legislative one was formed, and from that date the whole public revenue of Scotland tended towards London, towards which tended also, and necessarily, all who sought for place, power, or distinction. An absentee government produced, of course, absentee landholders, and with each step in this direction there was a diminution in the demand at home for talent, which thenceforward sought a market in the great city to which the rents were sent. The connection between the educated classes of Scotland and the Scottish seats of learning tended necessarily to decline, while the connection between the former and the universities of England became more intimate. These results were, of course, gradually produced, but, as is the case with the stone as it falls towards the earth, the attraction of centralization grew with the growth of the city that was built out of the contributions of distant provinces, while the counteracting power of the latter as steadily declined, and the greater the decline the more rapid does its progress now become. Seventy years after the date of the Union, Edinburgh was still a great literary capital, and could then offer to the world the names of numerous men of whose reputation any country of the world might have been proud: Burns and McPherson; Robertson and Hume; Blair and Kames; Reid, Smith, and Stewart; Monboddo, Playfair, and Boswell; and numerous others, whose reputation has survived to the present day. Thirty-five years later, its press furnished the world with the works of Jeffrey and Brougham; Stewart, Brown, and Chalmers; Scott, Wilson, and Joanna Baillie; and with those of many others whose reputation was less widely spread, among whom were Galt, Hogg, Lockhart, and Miss Ferrier, the authoress of "Marriage." The "Edinburgh Review" and "Blackwood's Magazine," then, to a great extent, represented Scottish men, and Scottish modes of thought. Looking now on the same field of action, it is difficult, from this distance, to discover more than two Scottish authors, Alison and Sir William Hamilton, the latter all "the more conspicuous and remarkable, as he now," says the "North British Review" (Feb. 1853), "stands so nearly alone in the ebb of literary activity in Scotland, which has been so apparent during this generation." McCulloch and Macaulay were both, I believe, born in Scotland, but in all else they are English. Glasgow has recently presented the world with a new poet, in the person of Alexander Smith, but, unlike Ramsay and Burns, there is nothing Scottish about him beyond his place of birth. "It is not," says one of his reviewers, "Scottish scenery, Scottish history, Scottish character, and Scottish social humor, that he represents or depicts. Nor is there," it continues, "any trace in him of that feeling of intense nationality so common in Scottish writers. London," as it adds, "a green lane in Kent, an English forest, an English manorhouse, these are the scenes where the real business of the drama is transacted."[1]

[Footnote 1: North British Review, Aug. 1863.]

The "Edinburgh Review" has become to all intents and purposes an English journal, and "Blackwood" has lost all those characteristics by which it was in former times distinguished from the magazines published south of the Tweed.

Seeing these facts, we can scarcely fail to agree with the Review already quoted, in the admission that there are "probably fewer leading individual thinkers and literary guides in Scotland at present than at any other period of its history since the early part of the last century," since the day when Scotland itself lost its individuality. The same journal informs us that "there is now scarcely an instance of a Scotchman holding a learned position in any other country," and farther says that "the small number of names of literary Scotchmen known throughout Europe for eminence in literature and science is of itself sufficient to show to how great an extent the present race of Scotchmen have lost the position which their ancestors held in the world of letters." [1]

[Footnote 1: North British Review, May, 1853.]

How, indeed, could it be otherwise? Centralization tends to carry to London all the wealth and all the expenditure of the kingdom, and thus to destroy everywhere the local demand for books or newspapers, or for men capable of producing either. Centralization taxes the poor people of the north of Scotland, and their complaints of distress are answered by an order for their expulsion, that place may be made for sheep and shepherds, neither of whom make much demand for books. Centralization appropriates millions for the improvement of London and the creation of royal palaces and pleasure-grounds in and about that city, while Holyrood, and all other of the buildings with which Scottish history is connected, are allowed to go to ruin. Centralization gives libraries and museums to London, but it refuses the smallest aid to the science or literature of Scotland. Centralization deprives the people of the power to educate themselves, by drawing from them more than thirty millions of dollars, raised by taxation, and it leaves the professors in the colleges of Scotland in the enjoyment of chairs, the emoluments of many of which are but $1,200 per annum. Whence, then, can come the demand for books, or the power to compensate the people who make them? Not, assuredly, from the mass of unhappy people who occupy the Highlands, whose starving condition furnishes so frequent occasion for the comments of their literary countrymen; nor, as certainly, from the wretched inhabitants of the wynds of Glasgow, or from the weavers of Paisley. Centralization is gradually separating the people into two classes—the very rich, who live in London, and the very poor, who remain in Scotland; and with the progress of this division there is a gradual decay in the feeling of national pride, that formerly so much distinguished the people of Scotland. The London "Leader" tells its readers that "England is a power made up of conquests over nationalities;" and it is right. The nationality of Scotland has disappeared; and, however much it may annoy our Scottish friends[1] to have the energetic and intelligent Celt sunk in the "slow and unimpressible" Saxon, such is the tendency of English centralization, everywhere destructive of that national feeling which is essential to progress in civilization.

[Footnote 1: See Blackwood's Magazine, Sept. 1853, art. "Scotland since the Union."]

Looking to Ireland, we find a similar state of things. Seventy years since, that country was able to insist upon and to establish its claim for an independent government, and, by aid of the measures then adopted, was rapidly advancing. From that period to the close of the century the demand for books for Ireland was so great as to warrant the republication of a large portion of those produced in England. The kingdom of Ireland of that day gave to the world such men as Burke and Grattan, Moore and Edgeworth, Curran, Sheridan, and Wellington. Centralization, however, demanded that Ireland should become a province of England, and from that time famines and pestilences have been of frequent occurrence, and the whole population is now being expelled to make room for the "slow and unimpressible" Saxon race. Under these circumstances, it is matter of small surprise that Ireland not only produces no books, but that she furnishes no market for those produced by others. Half a century of international copyright has almost annihilated both the producers and the consumers of books.

Passing towards England we may for a moment look to Wales, and then, if we desire to find the effects of centralization and its consequent absenteeism, in neglected schools, ignorant teachers, decaying and decayed churches, and drunken clergymen with immoral flocks, our object will be accomplished by studying the pages of the "Edinburgh Review" [2] In such a state of things as is there described there can be little tendency to the development of intellect, and little of either ability or inclination to reward the authors of books. In my next, I will look to England herself.

[Footnote 2: April, 1853, art. "The Church in the Mountains."]

LETTER IV.

Arrived in England, we find there everywhere the same tendency towards centralization. Of the 200,000 small landed proprietors of the days of Adam Smith but few remain, and of even those the number is gradually diminishing. Great landed estates have everywhere absentees for owners, agents for managers, and day laborers for workmen. The small landowner was a resident, and had a personal interest in the details of the neighborhood, not now felt by either the owner or the laborer. This state of things existed to a considerable extent five-and-thirty years ago, but it has since grown with great rapidity. At that time Great Britain could exhibit to the world perhaps as large a body of men and women of letters, with world-wide reputation, as ever before existed in any country or nation, as will be seen from the following list:—

Byron, Wilson, Clarkson,
Moore, Hallam, Landor,
Scott, Roscoe, Wellington,[1]
Wordsworth, Malthus, Robert Hall,
Rogers, Ricardo, Taylor,
Campbell, Mill, Romilly,
Joanna Baillie, Chalmers, Edgeworth,
Southey, Coleridge, Hannah More,
Gifford, Heber, Dalton,
Jeffrey, Bentham, Davy,
Sydney Smith, Brown, Wollaston,
Brougham, Mackintosh, The Herschels,
Horner, Stewart, Dr. Clarke.

[Footnote 1: Wellington's dispatches place him in the first rank of historians.]

DeQuincey was then just coming on the stage. Crabbe, Shelley, Keats, Croly, Hazlitt, Lockhart, Lamb, Hunt, Galt, Lady Morgan, Miss Mitford, Horace Smith, Hook, Milman, Miss Austen, and a host of others, were already on it. Many of these appear to have received rewards far greater than fall now to the lot of some of the most distinguished literary men. Crabbe is said to have received 3,000 guineas, or $15,000, for his "Tales of the Hall," and Theodore Hook 2,000 guineas for "Sayings and Doings," and, if the facts were so, they prove that poets and novelists were far more valued then than now. At that time, Croker, Barrow, and numerous other men of literary reputation co-operated with Southey and Gifford in providing for the pages of the "Quarterly." All these, men and women, were the product of the last century, when the small landholders of England yet counted by hundreds of thousands.

Since then, centralization has made great progress. The landholders now amount, as we are informed, to only 30,000, and the gulf which separates the great proprietor from the cultivator has gradually widened, as the one has become more an absentee and the other more a day laborer. The greater the tendency towards the absorption of land by the wealthy banker and merchant, or the wealthy cotton-spinner like Sir Robert Peel, the greater is the tendency towards its abandonment by the small proprietor, who has an interest in local self government, and the greater the tendency towards the centralization of power in London and in the great seats of manufacture. In all those places, it is thought that the prosperity of England is dependent upon "a cheap and abundant supply of labor."[1] The "Times" assures its readers that it is "to the cheap labor of Ireland that England is indebted for all her great works;" and that note is repeated by a large portion of the literary men of England who now ask for protection in the American market against the effects of the system they so generally advocate.

[Footnote 1: North British Review, November, 1852.]

The more the people of Scotland can be driven from the land to take refuge in Glasgow and Paisley, the cheaper must be labor. The more those of Ireland can be driven to England, the greater must be the competition in the latter for employment, and the lower must be the price of labor. The more the land of England can be centralized, the greater must be the mass of people seeking employment in London, Liverpool, Manchester, and Birmingham, and the cheaper must labor be.

Low-priced laborers cannot exercise self-government. All they earn is required for supplying themselves with indifferent food, clothing, and lodging, and they cannot control the expenditure of their wages to such extent as to enable them to educate their children, and hence it is that the condition of the people of England is as here described:—

"About one half of our poor can neither read nor write. The test of signing the name at marriage is a very imperfect absolute test of education, but it is a very good relative one: taking that test, how stands Leeds itself in the Registrar-General's returns? In Leeds, which is the centre of the movement for letting education remain as it is, left entirely to chance and charity to supply its deficiencies, how do we find the fact? This, that in 1846, the last year to which these returns are brought down, of 1,850 marriages celebrated in Leeds and Hunslet, 508 of the men and 1,020 of the women, or considerably more than one half of the latter, signed their names with marks. 'I have also a personal knowledge of this fact—that of 47 men employed upon a railway in this immediate neighborhood, only 14 can sign their names in the receipt of their wages; and this not because of any diffidence on their part, but positively because they cannot write.' And only lately, the "Leeds Mercury" itself gave a most striking instance of ignorance among persons from Boeotian Pudsey: of 12 witnesses, 'all of respectable appearance, examined before the Mayor of Bradford at the court-house there, only one man could sign his name, and that indifferently.' Mr. Neison has clearly shown, in statistics of crime in England and Wales from 1834 to 1844, that crime is invariably the most prevalent in those districts where the fewest numbers in proportion to the population can read and write. Is it not, indeed, beginning at the wrong end to try and reform men after they have become criminals? Yet you cannot begin with children, from want of schools. Poverty is the result of ignorance, and then ignorance is again the unhappy result of poverty. 'Ignorance makes men improvident and thoughtless—women as well as men; it makes them blind to the future— to the future of this life as well as the life beyond. It makes them dead to higher pleasures than those of the mere senses, and keeps them down to the level of the mere animal. Hence the enormous extent of drunkenness throughout this country, and the frightful waste of means which it involves.' At Bilston, amidst 20,000 people, there are but two struggling schools—one has lately ceased; at Millenhall, Darlaston, and Pelsall, amid a teeming population, no school whatever. In Oldham, among 100,000, but one public day-school for the laboring classes; the others are an infant-school, and some dame and factory schools. At Birmingham, there are 21,824 children at school, and 23,176 at no school; at Liverpool, 50,000 out of 90,000 at no school; at Leicester, 8,200 out of 12,500; and at Leeds itself, in 1841 (the date of the latest returns), some 9,600 out of 16,400 were at no school whatever. It is the same in the counties. 'I have seen it stated that a woman for some time had to officiate as clerk in a church in Norfolk, there being no adult male in the parish able to read and write.' For a population of 17,000,000 we have but twelve normal schools; while in Massachusetts they have three such schools for only 800,000 of population."

Poverty and ignorance produce intemperance and crime, and hence it is that both so much abound throughout England. Infanticide, as we are told, prevails to an extent unknown in any other part of the world. Looking at all these facts, we can readily see that the local demand for information throughout England must be very small, and this enables us to account for the extraordinary fact, that in all that country there has been no daily newspaper printed out of London. There is, consequently, no local demand for literary talent. The weekly papers that are published require little of the pen, but much of the scissors. The necessary consequence of this is, that every young man who fancies he can write, must go to London to seek a channel through which he may be enabled to come before the public. Here we have centralization again. Arrived in London, he finds a few daily papers, but only one, as we are told, that pays its expenses, and around each of them is a corps of writers and editors as ill-disposed to permit the introduction of any new laborers in their field as are the street-beggars of London to permit any interference with their "beat." If he desires to become contributor to the magazines, it is the same. To obtain the privilege of contributing his "cheap labor" to their pages, he must be well introduced, and if he make the attempt without such introduction he is treated with a degree of insolence scarcely to be imagined by any one not familiar with the "answers to correspondents" in London periodicals. If disposed to print a book he finds a very limited number of publishers, each one surrounded with his corps of authors and editors, and generally provided with a journal in which to have his own books well placed before the world. If, now, he succeeds in gaining favorable notice, he finds that he can obtain but a very small proportion of the price of his book, even if it sell, because centralization requires that all books shall be advertised in certain London journals that charge their own prices, and thus absorb the proceeds of no inconsiderable portion of the edition. Next, he finds the Chancellor of the Exchequer requiring a share of the proceeds of the book for permission to use paper, and further permission to advertise his work when printed.[1] Inquiring to what purpose are devoted the proceeds of all these taxes, he learns that the centralization which it is the object of the British cheap-labor policy to establish, requires the maintenance of large armies and large fleets which absorb more than all the profits of the commerce they protect. The bookseller informs him that he must take the risk of finding paper, and of paying the Chancellor of the Exchequer, and the "Times" and numerous other journals; that every editor will expect a copy; that the interests of science require that he, poor as he is, shall give no less than eleven copies to the public; and that the most that can be hoped for from the first edition is, that it will not bring him in debt. His book appears, but the price is high, for the reason that the taxes are heavy, and the general demand for books is small. Cheap laborers cannot buy books; soldiers and sailors cannot buy books; and thus does centralization diminish the market for literary talent while increasing the cost of bringing it before the world. Centralization next steps in, in the shape of circulating libraries, that, for a few guineas a year, supply books throughout the kingdom, and enable hundreds of copies to do the work that should be done by thousands, and hence it is that, while first editions of English works are generally small, so very few of them ever reach second ones. Popular as was Captain Marryat, his first editions were, as he himself informed me, for some time only 1,500, and had not then risen above 2,000. Of Mr. Bulwer's novels, so universally popular, the first edition never exceeded 2,500; and so it has been, and is, with others. With all Mr. Thackeray's popularity, the sale of his books has, I believe, rarely gone beyond 6,000 for the supply of above thirty millions of people. Occasionally, a single author is enabled to fix the attention of the public, and he is enabled to make a fortune—not from the sale of large quantities at low prices, but of moderate quantities at high prices. The chief case of the kind now in England is that of Mr. Dickens, who sells for twenty shillings a book that costs about four shillings and sixpence to make, and charges his fellow-laborers in the field of literature an enormous price for the privilege of attaching to his numbers the advertisements of their works, as is shown in the following paragraph from one of the journals of the day:—

"Thus far, no writer has succeeded in drawing so large pecuniary profits from the exercise of his talents as Charles Dickens. His last romance, "Bleak House," which appeared in monthly numbers, had so wide a circulation in that form that it became a valuable medium for advertising, so that before its close the few pages of the tale were completely lost in sheets of advertisements which were stitched to them. The lowest price for such an advertisement was £1 sterling, and many were paid for at the rate of £5 and £6. From this there is nothing improbable in the supposition that, in addition to the large sum received for the tale, its author gained some £15,000 by his advertising sheets. The "Household Words" produces an income of about £4,000, though Dickens, having put it entirely in the hands of an assistant editor, has nothing to do with it beyond furnishing a weekly article. Through his talents alone he has raised himself from the position of a newspaper reporter to that of a literary Croesus."

[Footnote 1: The tax on advertisements has just now been repealed, but that tax was a small one when compared with that imposed by centralization.]

Centralization produces the "cheap and abundant supply of labor" required for the maintenance of the British manufacturing system, and "cheap labor" furnishes Mr. Dickens with his "Oliver Twist," his "Tom-all-alone's," and the various other characters and situation by aid of whose delineation he is enabled, as a German writer informs us, to have dinners

"at which the highest aristocracy is glad to be present, and where he equals them in wealth, and furnishes an intellectual banquet of wit and wisdom which they, the highest and most refined circles, cannot imitate."

Centralization enables Mr. Dickens to obtain vast sums by advertising the works of the poor authors by whom he is surrounded, most of whom are not only badly paid, but insolently treated, while even of those whose names and whose works are well known abroad many gladly become recipients of the public charity. In the zenith of her reputation, Lady Charlotte Bury received, as I am informed, but £200 ($960) for the absolute copyright of works that sold for $7.50. Lady Blessington, celebrated as she was, had but from three to four hundred pounds; and neither Marryat nor Bulwer ever received, as I believe, the selling price of a thousand copies of their books as compensation for the copyright.[1] Such being the facts in regard to well-known authors, some idea may be formed in relation to the compensation of those who are obscure. The whole tendency of the "cheap labor" system, so generally approved by English writers, is to destroy the value of literary labor by increasing the number of persons who must look to the pen for means of support, and by diminishing the market for its products. What has been the effect of the system will now be shown by placing before you a list of the names of all existing British authors whose reputation can be regarded as of any wide extent, as follows:—

Tennyson, Thackeray, Grote, McCulloch,
Carlyle, Bulwer, Macaulay, Hamilton,
Dickens, Alison, J. S. Mill, Faraday.
[Footnote 1: This I had from Captain Marryat himself.]
This list is very small as compared with that presented in the same field five-and-thirty years since, and its difference in weight is still greater than in number. Scott, the novelist and poet, may certainly be regarded as the counterpoise of much more than any one of the writers of fiction in this list. Byron, Moore, Rogers, and Campbell enjoyed a degree of reputation far exceeding that of Tennyson. Wellington, the historian of his own campaigns, would much outweigh any of the historians. Malthus and Ricardo were founders of a school that has greatly influenced the policy of the world, whereas McCulloch and Mill are but disciples in that school. Dalton, Davy, and Wollaston will probably occupy a larger space in the history of science than Sir Michael Faraday, large, even, as may be that assigned to him.

Extraordinary as is the existence of such a state of things in a country claiming so much to abound in wealth, it is yet more extraordinary that we look around in vain to see who are to replace even these when age or death shall withdraw them from the literary world. Of all here named, Mr. Thackeray is the only one that has risen to reputation in the last ten years, and he is no longer young; and even he seeks abroad that reward for his efforts which is denied to him by the "cheap labor" system at home. Of the others, nearly, if not quite all, have been for thirty years before the world, and, in the natural course of things, some of them must disappear from the stage of authorship, if not of life. If we seek their successors among the writers for the weekly or monthly journals, we shall certainly fail to find them. Looking to the Reviews, we find ourselves forced to agree with the English journalist, who informs his readers that "it is said, and with apparent justice, that the quarterlies are not as good as they were." From year to year they have less the appearance of being the production of men who looked to any thing beyond mere pecuniary compensation for their labor. In reading them we find ourselves compelled to agree with the reviewer who regrets to see that the centralization which is hastening the decline of the Scottish universities is tending to cause the mind of the whole youth of Scotland to be

"Cast in the mould of English universities, institutions which, from their very completeness, exercise on second-rate minds an influence unfavorable to originality and power of thought."—North British Review, May 1853.

Their pupils are, as he says, struck "with one mental die," than which nothing can be less favorable to literary or scientific development.

Thirty years since, Sir Humphrey Davy spoke with his countrymen as follows:—

"There are very few persons who pursue science with true dignity; it is followed more as connected with objects of profit than fame."— Consolation in Travel.

Since then, Sir John Herschel has said to them:—

"Here whole branches of continental study are unstudied, and indeed almost unknown by name. It is in vain to conceal the melancholy truth. We are fast dropping behind."—Treatise on Sound.

A late writer, already quoted, says that learning is in disrepute. The English people, as he informs us, have

"No longer time or patience for the luxury of a learned treatment of their interests; and a learned lawyer or statesmen, instead of being eagerly sought for, is shunned as an impediment to public business."
—North British Review.

The reviewer is, as he informs us, "far from regarding this tendency, unfavorable as it is to present progress, as a sign of social retrogression." He thinks that

"Reference to general principles for rules of immediate action on the part of those actually engaged in the dispatch of business, must, from the delay which it necessarily occasions, come to be regarded as a worse evil than action which is at variance with principle altogether."

Demand tends to procure supply. Destroy the demand, and the supply will cease. Science, whether natural or social, is not in demand in Great Britain, and hence the diminution of supply. We have here the secret of literary and scientific decline, so obvious to all who study English books or journals, or read the speeches of English statesmen. Empiricism prevails everywhere, and there is a universal disposition to avoid the study of principles. The "cheap labor" system, which it is the object of the whole British policy to establish, cannot be defended on principle, and therefore principles are avoided. Centralization, cheap labor, and enslavement of the body and the mind, travel always in company, and with each step of their progress there is an increasing tendency towards the accumulation of power in the hands of men who should be statesmen, the difficulties of whose positions forbid, however, that they should refer to scientific principles for their government. Action must be had, and immediate action in opposition to principle is preferable to delay; and hence it is that real statesmen are "shunned as an impediment to public business." The greater the necessity for statesmanship, the more must statesmen be avoided. The nearer the ship is brought to the shoal, the more carefully must her captain avoid any reference to the chart. That such is the practice of those charged with the direction of the affairs of England, and such the philosophy of those who control her journals, is obvious to all who study the proceedings of the one or the teachings of the other. From year to year the ship becomes more difficult of management, and there is increasing difficulty in finding responsible men to take the helm. Such are the effects upon mind that have resulted from that "destruction of nationalities" required for the perfection of the British system of centralization.

England is fast becoming one great shop, and traders have, in general, neither time nor disposition to cultivate literature. The little proprietors disappear, and the day laborers who succeed them can neither educate their children nor purchase books. The great proprietor is an absentee, and he has little time for either literature or science. From year to year the population of the kingdom becomes more and more divided into two great classes; the very poor, with whom food and raiment require all the proceeds of labor, and the very rich who prosper by the cheap labor system, and therefore eschew the study of principles. With the one class, books are an unattainable luxury, while with the other the absence of leisure prevents the growth of desire for their purchase. The sale is, therefore, small; and hence it is that authors are badly paid. In strong contrast with the limited sale of English books at home, is the great extent of sale here, as shown in the following facts: Of the octavo edition of the "Modern British Essayists," there have been sold in five years no less than 80,000 volumes. Of Macaulay's "Miscellanies," 3 vols. 12mo., the sale has amounted to 60,000 volumes. Of Miss Aguilar's writings, the sale, in two years, has been 100,000 volumes. Of Murray's "Encyclopedia of Geography," more than 50,000 volumes have been sold, and of McCulloch's "Commercial Dictionary," 10,000 volumes. Of Alexander Smith's poems, the sale, in a few months, has reached 10,000 copies. The sale of Mr. Thackeray's works has been quadruple that of England, and that of the works of Mr. Dickens counts almost by millions of volumes. Of "Bleak House," in all its various forms— in newspapers, magazines, and volumes—it has already amounted to several hundred thousands of copies. Of Bulwer's last novel, since it was completed, the sale has, I am told, exceeded 35,000. Of Thiers's "French Revolution and Consulate," there have been sold 32,000, and of Montagu's edition of Lord Bacon's works 4,000 copies.

If the sales of books were as great in England as they are here, English authors would be abundantly paid. In reply it will be said their works are cheap here because we pay no copyright. For payment of the authors, however, a very small sum would be required, if the whole people of England could afford, as they should be able to do, to purchase books. A contribution of a shilling per head would give, as has been shown, a sum of almost eight millions of dollars, sufficient to pay to fifteen hundred salaries nearly equal to those of our Secretaries of State. Centralization, however, destroys the market for books, and the sale is, therefore, small; and the few successful writers owe their fortunes to the collection of large contributions made among a small number of readers; while the mass of authors live on, as did poor Tom Hood, from day to day, with scarcely a hope of improvement in their condition.

Sixty years since, Great Britain was a wealthy country, abounding in libraries and universities, and giving to the world some of the best, and best paid, writers of the age. At that time the people of this country were but four millions, and they were poor, while unprovided with either books or libraries. Since then they have grown to twenty-six millions, millions of whom have been emigrants, in general arriving here with nothing but the clothing on their backs. These poor men have had every thing to create for themselves—farms, roads, houses, libraries, schools, and colleges; and yet, poor as they have been, they furnish now a demand for the principal products of English mind greater than is found at home. If we can make such a market, why cannot they? If they had such a market, would it not pay their authors to the full extent of their merits? Unquestionably it would; and if they see fit to pursue a system tending to cheapen the services of the laborer in the field, in the workshop, and at the desk, there is no more reason for calling upon the people of this country to make up their deficiencies towards those who contribute to their pleasure or instruction by writing books, than there would be in asking us to aid in supporting the hundreds of thousands of day laborers, their wives and children, whom the same system condemns, unpitied, to the workhouse.

But, it will be asked, is it right that we should read the works of Macaulay, Dickens, and others, without compensation to the authors? In answer, it may be said, that we give them precisely what their own countrymen have given to their Dalton, Davy, Wollaston, Franklin, Parry, and the thousands of others who have furnished the bodies of which books are composed— and more than we ourselves give to the men among us engaged in cultivating science—fame. This, it will be said, is an unsubstantial return; yet Byron deemed it quite sufficient when he first saw an American edition of his works, coming, as it seemed to him, "from posterity." Miss Bremer found no small reward for her labors in knowing the high regard in which she was held; and it was no small payment when, even in the wilds of the West, she met with numerous persons who would gladly have her travel free of charge, because of the delight she had afforded them. Miss Carlen tells her readers that "of one triumph" she was proud. "It was," she says, "when I held in my hand, for the first time, one of my works, translated and published in America. My eyes filled with tears. The bright dreams of youth again passed before me. Ye Americans had planted the seed, and ye also approved of the fruit!" This is the feeling of a writer that cultivates literature with some object in view other than mere profit. It differs entirely from that of English authors, because in England, more than in any other country, book-making is a trade, carried on exclusively with a view to profit; and hence it is that the character of English books so much declines.

But is it really true that foreign authors derive no pecuniary advantage from

the republication of their books in this country? It is not. Mr. Macaulay has admitted that much of his reputation, and of the sale of his books at home, had been a consequence of his reputation here, where his Essays were first reprinted. At the moment of writing this, I have met with a notice of his speeches, first collected here, from which the following is an extract:—
"We owe much to America. Not content with charming us with the works of her native genius, she teaches us also to appreciate our own. She steps in between the timidity of a British author, and the fastidiousness of the British public, and by using her' good offices' brings both parties to a friendly understanding."—Morning Chronicle.
If the people of England are largely indebted to America for being made acquainted with the merits of their authors, are not these latter also indebted to America for much of their pecuniary reward? Undoubtedly they are. Mr. Macaulay owes much of his fortune to American publishers, readers, and critics; and such is the case to perhaps a greater extent with Mr. Carlyle, whose papers were first collected here, and their merits thus made known to his countrymen. Lamb's papers of "Elia" were first collected here. It is to the diligence of an American publisher that De Quincey owes the publication of a complete edition of his works, now to be followed by a similar one in England. The papers of Professor Wilson owe their separate republication to American booksellers. The value of Mr. Thackeray's copyrights has been greatly increased by his reception here. So has it been with Mr. Dickens. All of those persons profit largely by their fame abroad, while the men who contribute to the extension of knowledge by the publication of facts and ideas never reap profit from their publication abroad, and are rarely permitted to acquire even fame. Godfrey died poor. The merchants of England gave no fortune to his children, and Hadley stole his fame. The people of that country, who travel in steam-vessels, have given to the family of Fulton no pecuniary reward, while her writers have uniformly endeavored to deprive him of the reputation which constituted almost the sole inheritance of his family. The whole people of Europe are profiting by the discovery of chloroform; but who inquires what has become of the family of its unfortunate discoverer? Nobody! The people of England profit largely by the discoveries of Fourcroy, Berzelius, and many other of the continental philosophers; but do those who manufacture cheap cloth, or those who wear it, contribute to the support of the families of those philosophers? Did they contribute to their support while alive? Certainly not. To do so would have been in opposition to the idea that the real contributors to knowledge should be "hewers of wood and drawers of water" for the gentlemen who dress up their facts and ideas in an attractive form and place them before the world in the form of cloth or books.
We are largely indebted to the labors of literary men, and they should be

well paid, but their claims to pecuniary reward have been much exaggerated, because they have held the pen and have had always a high degree of belief in their own deserts. Their right in the books they publish is precisely similar to, and no greater than, that of the man who culls the flowers and arranges the bouquets; and, when that is provided for, their books are entitled to become common property. English authors are already secured in a monopoly for forty-two years among a body of people so large that a contribution of a shilling a head would enable each and all of them to live in luxury; and if British policy prevents their countrymen from paying them, it is to the British Parliament they should look for redress, and not to our Executive. When they shall awaken to the fact that "cheap labor" with the spade, the plough, and the loom, brings with it necessarily "cheap labor" with the pen, they will become opponents, and cease to be advocates of the system under which they suffer. All that, in the mean time, we can say to them is, that we protect our own authors by giving them a monopoly of our own immense and rapidly growing market, and that if they choose to come and live among us we will grant them the same protection. We may now look to the condition of our own literary men.

LETTER V.

Our system is based upon an idea directly the reverse of the one on which rests the English system—that of decentralization; and we may now study its effects as shown in the development of literary tendencies and in the reward of authors.

Centralization tends towards taxing the people for building up great institutions at a distance from those who pay the taxes; decentralization towards leaving to the people to tax themselves for the support of common and high schools in their immediate neighborhood. The first tends towards placing the man who has instruction to sell at a distance from those who need to buy it; while the other tends towards bringing the teacher to the immediate vicinity of the scholars, and thus diminishing the cost of education. The effects of the latter are seen in the fact that the new States, no less than the old ones, are engaged in an effort to enable all, without distinction of sex or fortune, to obtain the instruction needful for enabling them to become consumers of books, and customers to the men who produce them. Massachusetts exhibits to the world 182,000 scholars in her public schools; New York, 778,000 in the public ones, and 75,000 in the private ones; and Iowa and Wisconsin are laying the foundation of a system that will enable them, at a future day, to do as much. Boston taxes herself $365,000 for purposes of education, while Philadelphia expends more than half a million for the same purposes, and exhibits 50,000 children in her public schools. Here we have, at once, a great demand for instructors, offering a premium on intellectual effort, and its effect is seen in the numerous associations of teachers, each anxious to confer with the others in regard to improvement in the modes of education. School libraries are needed for the children, and already those of New York exhibit about a million and a half of volumes. Books of a higher class are required for the teachers, and here is created another demand leading to the preparation of new and improved books by the teachers themselves. The scholars enter life and next we find numerous apprentices' libraries and mercantile libraries, producing farther demand for books, and aiding in providing reward for those to whom the world is indebted for them. Everybody must learn to read and write, and everybody must therefore have books; and to this universality of demand it is due that the sale of those required for early education is so immense. Of the works of Peter Parley it counts by millions; but if we take his three historical books (price 75 cents each) alone, we find that it amounts to between half a million and a million of volumes. Of Goodrich's United States it has been a quarter of a million. Of Morse's Geography and Atlas (50 cents) the sale is said to be no less than 70,000 per annum. Of Abbott's histories the sale is said to have already been more than 400,000, while of Emerson's Arithmetic and Reader it counts almost by millions. Of Mitchell's several geographies it is 400,000 a year.

In other branches of education the same state of things is seen to exist. Of the Boston Academy's collection of sacred music the sale has exceeded 600,000; and the aggregate sale of five books by the same author has probably exceeded a million, at a dollar per volume. Leaving the common schools we come to the high schools and colleges, of which latter the names of no less than 120 are given in the American Almanac. Here again we have decentralization, and its effect is to bring within reach of almost the whole people a higher degree of education than could be afforded by the common schools. The problem to be solved is, as stated by a recent and most enlightened traveller, "How are citizens to be made thinking beings in the greatest numbers?" Its solution is found in making of the educational fabric a great pyramid, of which the common schools form the base and the Smithsonian Institute the apex, the intermediate places being filled with high schools, lyceums, and colleges of various descriptions, fitted to the powers and the means of those who need instruction. All these make, of course, demand for books, and hence it is that the sale of Anthon's series of classics (averaging $1) amounts, as I am told, to certainly not less than 50,000 volumes per annum, while of the "Classical Dictionary" of the same author ($4) not less than thirty thousand have been sold. Of Liddell and Scott's "Greek Lexicon" ($5), edited by Prof. Drisler, the sale has been not less than 25,000, and probably much larger. Of Webster's 4to. "Dictionary" ($6) it has been, I am assured, 60,000, and perhaps even 80,000; and of the royal 8vo. one ($3.50), 250,000. Of Bolmar's French school books not less than 150,00 volumes have been sold. The number of books used in the higher schools—text-books in philosophy, chemistry, and other branches of science—is exceedingly great, and it would be easy to produce numbers of which the sale is from five to ten thousand per annum; but to do so would occupy too much space, and I must content myself with the few facts already given in regard to this department of literature.

Decentralization, or local self-government, tends thus to place the whole people in a condition to read newspapers, while the same cause tends to produce those local interests which give interest to the public journals, and induce men to purchase them. Hence it is that their number is so large. The census of 1850 gives it at 2,625; and the increase since that time has been very great. The total number of papers printed can scarcely be under 600,000,000, which would give almost 24 for every person, old and young, black and white, male and female, in the Union. But recently the newspaper press of the United Kingdom was said to require about 160,000 reams of paper, which would give about 75,000,000 of papers, or two and a half per head.

The number of daily papers was returned at 350, but it has greatly increased, and must now exceed four hundred. Chicago, which then was a small town, rejoices now in no less than 24 periodicals, seven of which are daily, and five of them of the largest size. At St. Louis, which but a few years since was on the extreme borders of civilization, we find several, and one of these has grown from a little sheet of 8 by 12 inches to the largest size, yielding to its proprietors $50,000 per annum, while Liverpool, Manchester, and Birmingham are still compelled to depend upon their tri-weekly sheets. St. Louis itself furnishes the type, and Louisville furnishes the paper. Everywhere, the increase in size is greater than that in the number of newspapers, and the increase of ability in both the city and country press, greater than in either number or size. These things are necessary consequences of that decentralization which builds school-houses and provides teachers, where centralization raises armies and provides generals. The schools enable young men to read, think, and write, and the local newspaper is always at hand in which to publish. Beginning thus with the daily or weekly journal, the youth of talent makes his way gradually to the monthly or quarterly magazine, and ultimately to the independent book. Examine where we may through the newspaper press, there is seen the activity which always accompanies the knowledge that men can rise in the world if they will; but this is particularly obvious in the daily press of cities, whose efforts to obtain information, and whose exertions to lay it before the public, are without a parallel. Centralization, like that of the London "Times," furnishes its readers with brief paragraphs of telegraphic news, where decentralization gives columns. The New York "Tribune" furnishes, for two cents, better papers than are given in London for ten, and it scatters them over the country by hundreds of thousands. Decentralization is educating the whole mind of the country, and it is to this it is due that the American farmer is furnished with machines which are, according to the London "Times," "about twice as light in draught as the lightest of English machines of the same description, doing as much, if not more work than the best of them, and with much less power; dressing the grain, which they do not, and which can be profitably disposed of at one half, or at least one third less money than its British rivals"—and is thus enabled to purchase books. Centralization, on the other hand, furnishes the English farmer, according to the same authority, "with machines strong and dear enough to rob him of all future improvements, and tremendously heavy, either to work or to draw;" and thus deprives him of all power to educate his children, or to purchase for himself either books or newspapers.

Religious decentralization exerts also a powerful influence on the arrangements for imparting that instruction which provides purchasers for books. The Methodist Society, with its gigantic operations; the Presbyterian Board of Publication; the Baptist Association; the Sunday-school, and other societies, are all incessantly at work creating readers. The effect of all these efforts for the dissemination of cheap knowledge is shown in the first instance in the number of semi-monthly, monthly, and quarterly journals, representing every shade of politics and religion, and every department of literature and science.

The number of these returned to the census was 175; but that must, I think, have been even then much below the truth. Since then it has been much increased. Of two of them, Putnam's and Harper's, the first exclusively original, and the latter about two thirds so, the sale is about two millions of numbers per annum; while of three others, published in Philadelphia, it is about a million. Cheap as are these journals, at twenty-five cents each, the sum total of the price paid for them by the consumers is about $700,000. The quantity of paper required for a single one of them is about 16,000 reams of double medium, being one tenth as much as has recently been given as the consumption of the whole newspaper press of Great Britain and Ireland. Every pursuit in life, and almost every shade of opinion, has its periodical. A single city in Western New York furnishes no less than four agricultural and horticultural journals, one of them published weekly, with a circulation of 15,000, and the others, monthly, with a joint circulation of 25,000. The "Merchants' Magazine," which set the example for the one now published in London, has a circulation of 3,500. The "Bankers' Magazine" also set the example recently followed in England. Medicine and Law have their numerous and well supported journals; and Dental Surgery alone has five, one of which has a circulation of 5,000 copies, while all Europe has but two, and those of very inferior character.[1] North, south, east, and west, the periodical press is collecting the opinions of all our people, while centralization is gradually limiting the expression of opinion, in England, to those who live in and near London. Upon this extensive base of cheap domestic literature rests that portion of the fabric composed of reproduction of foreign books, the quantities of some of which were given in my last. The proportion which these bear to American books has been thus given for the six months ending on the 30th of June last:

Republications 169

Original 522

691

[Footnote 1: It is a remarkable fact that there should be in this country no less than four Colleges of Dental Surgery, while all Europe presents not even a single one.]

Of these last, 17 were original translations.

We see, thus, that the proportion of domestic to foreign products is already more than three to one. How the sale of the latter compares with that of the former, will be seen by the following facts in relation to books of almost all sizes, prices, and kinds; some of which have been furnished by the publishers themselves, whilst others are derived from gentlemen connected with the trade whose means of information are such as warrant entire reliance upon their statements.

Of all American authors, those of school-books excepted, there is no one of whose books so many have been circulated as those of Mr. Irving. Prior to the publication of the edition recently issued by Mr. Putnam, the sale had amounted to some hundreds of thousands; and yet of that edition, selling at $1.25 per volume, it has already amounted to 144,000 vols. Of "Uncle Tom," the sale has amounted to 295,000 copies, partly in one, and partly in two volumes, and the total number of volumes amounts probably to about 450,000.

Price per vol. Volumes.

Of the two works of Miss Warner, Queechy, and the Wide, Wide World, the price and sale have been. $ 88 104,000

Fern Leaves, by Fanny Fern, in six months. 1 25 45,000

Reveries of a Bachelor, and other books, by Ike Marvel. 1 25 70,000

Alderbrook, by Fanny Forester, 3 vols. 50 33,000

Northup's Twelve Years a Slave 1 00 20,000

Novels of Mrs. Hentz, in three years 63 93,000

Major Jones' Courtship and Travels 50 31,000

Salad for the Solitary, by a new author,

in five months 1 25 5,000

Headley's Napoleon and his Marshals, Washington

and his Generals, and other works. 1 25 200,000

Stephen's Travels in Egypt and Greece. 87 80,000

" " Yucatan and Central America 2 50 60,000

Kendall's Expedition to Santa Fe 1 25 40,000
Lynch's Expedition to the Dead Sea, 8vo. $3 00 15,000
" " 2mo. 1 25 8,000
Western Scenes 2 50 14,000
Young's Science of Government 1 00 12,000
Seward's Life of John Quincy Adams. 1 00 30,000
Frost's Pictorial History of the World, 3 vols. 2 50 60,000
Sparks' American Biography, 25 vols 75 100,000
Encyclopaedia Americana, 14 vols. 2 00 280,000
Griswold's Poets and Prose Writers
of America, 3 vols. 3 00 21,000
Barnes' Notes on the Gospels, Epistles, andc.,
11 vols. 75 300.000
Aiken's Christian Minstrel, in two years. 62 40,000
Alexander on the Psalms, 3 vols. 1 17 10,000
Buist's Flower Garden Directory 1 25 10,000
Cole on Fruit Trees. 50 18,000
" Diseases of Domestic Animals 50 34,000
Downing's Fruits and Fruit Trees. 50 15,000
" Rural Essays. 3 50 3,000
" Landscape Gardening. 3 50 9,000
" Cottage Residences. 2 00 6,250
" Country Homes. 4 00 3,500
Mahan's Civil Engineering. 3 00 7,500
Leslie's Cookery and Receipt-books. 1 00 96,000
Guyot's Lectures on Earth and Man. 1 00 6,000
Wood and Bache's Medical Dispensatory 5 00 60,000
Dunglison's Medical Writings, in all 10 vols. 2 50 50,000
Pancoast's Surgery, 4to. 10 00 4,000
Rayer, Ricord, and Moreau's Surgical Works (translations). 15 00 5,500
Webster's Works, 6 vols. 2 00 46,800
Kent's Commentaries, 4 vols. 3 38 84,000
Next to Chancellor Kent's work comes Greenleaf on Evidence, 3 vols., $16.50; the sale of which has been exceedingly great, but what has been its extent, I cannot say.

Of Blatchford's General Statutes of New York, a local work, price $4.50, the sale has been 3,000; equal to almost 30,000 of a similar work for the United Kingdom.

How great is the sale of Judge Story's books can be judged only from the fact that the copyright now yields, and for years past has yielded, more than $8,000 per annum. Of the sale of Mr. Prescott's works little is certainly known, but it cannot, I understand, have been less than 160,000 volumes. That of Mr. Bancroft's History, has already risen, certainly to 30,000 copies, and I am told it is considerably more; and yet even that is a sale, for such a work, entirely unprecedented.

Of the works of Hawthorne, Longfellow, Bryant, Willis, Curtis, Sedgwick, Sigourney, and numerous others, the sale is exceedingly great; but, as not even an approximation to the true amount can be offered, I must leave it to you to judge of it by comparison with those of less popular authors above enumerated. In several of these cases, beautifully illustrated editions have been published, of which large numbers have been sold. Of Mr. Longfellow's volume there have been no less than ten editions. These various facts will probably suffice to satisfy you that this country presents a market for books of almost every description, unparalleled in the world.

In reflecting upon this subject, it is necessary to bear in mind that the monopoly, granted to authors and their families, is for the term of no less than forty-two years, and that in that period the number of persons subjected to it is likely to grow to little short of a hundred millions, with a power of consumption that will probably be ten times greater than now exists. If the Commentaries of Chancellor Kent continue to maintain their present position, as they probably will, may we not reasonably suppose that the demand for them will continue as great, or nearly so, as it is at present, and that the total sale during the period of copyright will reach a quarter of a million of volumes? So, too, of the histories of Bancroft and Prescott, and of other books of permanent character.

Such being the extent of the market for the products of literary labor, we may now inquire into its rewards.

Beginning with the common schools, we find a vast number of young men and young women acting as teachers of others, while qualifying themselves for occupying other places in life. Many of them rise gradually to become teachers in high schools and professors in colleges, while all of them have at hand the newspaper, ready to enable them, if gifted with the power of expressing themselves on paper, to come before the world. The numerous newspapers require editors and contributors, and the amount appropriated to the payment of this class of the community is a very large one. Next come the magazines, many of which pay very liberally. I have now before me a statement from a single publisher, in which he says that to Messrs. Willis, Longfellow, Bryant, and Alston, his price was uniformly $50 for a poetical article, long or short—and his readers know that they were generally very short; in one case only fourteen lines. To numerous others it was from $25 to $40. In one case he has paid $25 per page for prose. To Mr. Cooper he paid $1,800 for a novel, and $1,000 for a series of naval biographies, the author retaining the copyright for separate publication; and in such cases, if the work be good, its appearance in the magazine acts as the best of advertisements. To Mr. James he paid $1,200 for a novel, leaving him also the copyright. For a single number of the journal he has paid to authors $1,500. The total amount paid for original matter by two magazines—the selling price of which is $3 per annum—in ten years, has exceeded $130,000, giving an average of $13,000 per annum. The Messrs. Harper inform me that the expenditure for literary and artistic labor required for their magazine is $2,000 per month, or $24,000 a year.

Passing upwards, we reach the producers of books, and here we find rewards not, I believe, to be paralleled elsewhere. Mr. Irving stands, I imagine, at the head of living authors for the amount received for his books. The sums paid to the renowned Peter Parley must have been enormously great, but what has been their extent I have no means of ascertaining. Mr. Mitchell, the geographer, has realized a handsome fortune from his schoolbooks. Professor Davies is understood to have received more than $50,000 from the series published by him. The Abbotts, Emerson, and numerous other authors engaged in the preparation of books for young persons and schools, are largely paid. Professor Anthon, we are informed, has received more than $60,000 for his series of classics. The French series of Mr. Bolmar has yielded him upwards of $20,000. The school geography of Mr. Morse is stated to have yielded more than $20,000 to the author. A single medical book, of one 8vo. volume, is understood to have produced its authors $60,000, and a series of medical books has given to its author probably $30,000. Mr. Downing's receipts from his books have been very large. The two works of Miss Warner must have already yielded her from $12,000 to $15,000, and perhaps much more. Mr. Headley is stated to have received about $40,000; and the few books of Ike Marvel have yielded him about $20,000; a single one, "The Reveries of a Bachelor," produced more than $4,000 in the first six months. Mrs. Stowe has been very largely paid. Miss Leslie's Cookery and Receipt books have paid her $12,000. Dr. Barnes is stated to have received more than $30,000 for the copyright of his religious works. Fanny Fern has probably received not less than $6,000 for the 12mo. volume published but six months since. Mr. Prescott was stated, several years since, to have then received $90,000 from his books, and I have never seen it contradicted. According to the rate of compensation generally understood to be received by Mr. Bancroft, the present sale of each volume of his yields him more than $15,000, and he has the long period of forty-two years for future sale. Judge Story died, as has been stated, in the receipt of more than $8,000 per annum; and the amount has not, as it is understood, diminished. Mr. Webster's works, in three years, can scarcely have paid less than $25,000. Kent's Commentaries are understood to have yielded to their author and his heirs more than $120,000, and if we add to this for the remainder of the period only one half of this sum, we shall obtain $180,000, or $45,000 as the compensation for a single 8vo. volume, a reward for literary labor unexampled in history. What has been the amount received by Professor Greenleaf I cannot learn, but his work stands second only, in the legal line, to that of Chancellor Kent. The price paid for Webster's 8vo. Dictionary is understood to be fifty cents per copy; and if so, with a sale of 250,000, it must already have reached $125,000. If now to this we add the quarto, at only a dollar a copy, we shall have a sum approaching to, and perhaps exceeding, $180,000; more, probably, than has been paid for all the dictionaries of Europe in the same period of time. What have been the prices paid to Messrs. Hawthorne, Longfellow, Bryant, Willis, Curtis, and numerous others, I cannot say; but it is well known that they have been very large. It is not, however, only the few who are liberally paid; all are so who manifest any ability, and here it is that we find the effect of the decentralizing system of this country as compared with the centralizing one of Great Britain. There Mr. Macaulay is largely paid for his Essays, while men of almost equal ability can scarcely obtain the means of support. Dickens is a literary Croesus, and Tom Hood dies leaving his family in hopeless poverty. Such is not here the case. Any manifestation of ability is sure to produce claimants for the publication of books. No sooner had the story of "Hot Corn" appeared in "The Tribune," than a dozen booksellers were applicants to the author for a book. The competition is here for the purchase of the privilege of printing, and this competition is not confined to the publishers of a single city, as is the case in Britain. Boston, New York, Philadelphia, and even Auburn and Cincinnati, present numerous publishers, all anxious to secure the works of writers of ability, in any department of literature; and were it possible to present a complete list of our well-paid authors, its extent could not fail to surprise you greatly, as the very few facts that have come to my knowledge in reference to some of the lesser stars of the literary world have done by me. You will observe that I have confined myself to the question of demand for books and compensation to their authors, without reference to that of the ability displayed in their preparation. That we may have good books, all that is required is that we make a large market for them, which is done here to an extent elsewhere unknown.

Forty years since, the question was asked by the "Edinburgh Review," Who reads an American book? Judging from the facts here given, may we not reasonably suppose that the time is fast approaching, when the question will be asked, Who does not read American books?

Forty years since, had we asked where were the homes of American authors, we should generally have been referred to very humble houses in our cities. Those who now inquire for them will find their answer in the beautiful volume lately published by Messrs. Putnam and Co., the precursor of others destined to show the literary men of this country enjoying residences as agreeable as any that had been occupied by such men in any part of the world; and in almost every case, those homes have been due to the profits of the pen. Less than half a century since, the race of literary men was scarcely known in the country, and yet the amount now paid for literary labor is greater than in Great Britain and France combined, and will probably be, in twenty years more, greater than in all the world beside. With the increase of number, there has been a corresponding increase in the consideration in which they are held; and the respect with which even unknown authors are treated, when compared with the disrespect manifested in England towards such men, will be obvious to all familiar with the management of the journals of that country who read the following in one of our principal periodicals:—

"The editor of Putnam's Monthly will give to every article forwarded for insertion in the Magazine a careful examination, and, when requested to do so, will return the MS. if not accepted."

Here, the competition is among the publishers to buy the products of literary labor, whereas, abroad, the competition is to sell them, and therefore is the treatment of our authors, even when unknown, so different. Long may it continue to be so!

Such having been the result of half a century, during which we have had to lay the foundation of the system that has furnished so vast a body of readers, what may not be expected in the next half century, during which the population will increase to a hundred millions, with a power to consume the products of literary labor growing many times faster than the growth of numbers? If this country is properly termed "the paradise of women," may it not be as correctly denominated the paradise of authors, and should they not be content to dwell in it as their predecessors have done? Is it wise in them to seek a change? Their best friends would, I think, unite with me in advising that it is not. Should they succeed in obtaining what they now desire, the day will, as I think, come, when they will be satisfied that their real friends had been, those who opposed the confirmation of the treaty now before the Senate.

LETTER VI.

We have commenced the erection of a great literary and scientific edifice. The foundation is already broad, deep, and well laid, but it is seen to increase in breadth, depth, and strength, with every step of increase in height; and the work itself is seen to assume, from year to year, more and more the natural form of a true pyramid. To the height that such a building may be carried, no living man will venture to affix a limit. What is the tendency to durability in a work thus constructed, the pyramids of Egypt and the mountains of the Andes and of the Himalaya may attest. That edifice is the product of decentralization.

Elsewhere, centralization is, as has been shown, producing the opposite effect, narrowing the base, and diminishing the elevation. Having prospered under decentralization, our authors seek to introduce centralization. Failing to accomplish their object by the ordinary course of legislation, they have had recourse to the executive power; and thus the end to be accomplished, and the means used for its accomplishment, are in strict accordance with each other.

We are invited to grant to the authors and booksellers of England, and their agent or agents here, entire control over a highly important source from which our people have been accustomed to derive their supplies of literary food. Before granting to these persons any power here, it might be well to inquire how they have used their power at home. Doing this, we find that, as is usually the case with those enjoying a monopoly, they have almost uniformly preferred to derive their profits from high prices and small sales, and have thus, in a great degree, deprived their countrymen of the power to purchase books; a consequence of which has been that the reading community has, very generally, been driven to dependence upon circulating libraries, to the injury of both the authors and the public. The extent to which this system of high prices in regard to school-books has been carried, and the danger of intrusting such men with power, are well shown in the fact that the same government which has so recently concluded a copyright treaty with our own, has since entered "into the bookselling trade on its own account," competing "with the private dealer, who has to bear copyright charges." The subjects of this "reactionary step" on the part of a government that so much professes to love free trade, are, as we are told, "the famous school-books of the Irish national system."[1] A new office has been created, "paid for with a public salary," for "the issue of books to the retail dealers;" and the centralization of power over this important portion to the trade is, we are told,[2] defended in the columns of the "Times," as "tending to bring down the price of school-books; for booksellers who possess copyrights, now sell their books at exorbitant prices, and, by underselling them, the commissioners will be able to beat them." Judging from this, it would seem almost necessary, if this treaty is to be ratified, that there should be added some provision authorizing our government to appoint commissioners for the regulation of trade, and for "underselling" those persons who "now sell their books at exorbitant prices." If it be ratified, we shall be only entering on the path of centralization; and it may not be amiss that, before ratification, we should endeavor to determine to what point it will probably carry us in the end.

[Footnote 1: Spectator, June 4, 1853.]

[Footnote 2: Ibid.]

The question is often asked, What difference can it make to the people of this country whether they do, or do not, pay to the English author a few cents in return for the pleasure afforded by the perusal of his book? Not very much, certainly, to the wealthy reader; but as every extra cent is important to the poorer one, and tends to limit his power to purchase, it may be well to calculate how many cents would probably be required; and, that we may do so, I give you here a list[1] of the comparative prices of English and American editions of a few of the books that have been published within the last few years:—

English. Amer.

Brande's Encyclopaedia $15 00 $4 00
Ure's Dictionary of Manufactures 15 00 5 00
Alison's Europe, cheapest edition 25 00 5 00
D'Aubignd's Reformation 11 50 2 25
Bulwer's "My Novel" 10 50 75
Lord Mahon's England 13 00 4 00
Macaulay's England, per vol. 4 50 40
Campbell's Chief Justices. 7 50 3 50
" Lord Chancellors 25 50 12 00
Queens of England, 8 vols. 24 00 10 00
Queens of Scotland 15 00 6 00
Hallam's Middle Ages 7 50 1 75
Arnold's Rome 12 00 3 00
Life of John Foster 6 00 1 25
Layard's Nineveh, complete edition. 9 00 1 75
Mrs. Somerville's Physical Sciences 2 50 50
Whewell's Elements of Morality. 7 50 1 00
Napier's Peninsular War 12 00 3 25
Thirlwall's Greece, cheapest edition 7 00 3 00
Dick's Practical Astronomer 2 50 50
Jane Eyre 7 50 25

[Footnote 1: Copied from an article in the New York Daily Times.]

The difference, as we see, between the selling price in London and in New York, of the first book in this list, is no less than eleven dollars, or almost three times as much as the whole price of the American edition. To what is this extraordinary difference to be attributed? To any excess in the cost of paper or printing in London? Certainly not; for paper and printers' labor are both cheaper there than here. Is it, then, to the necessity for compensating the author? Certainly not; for there are in this country fifty persons as fully competent as Mr. Brande for the preparation of such a work, who would willingly do it for a dollar a copy, calculating upon being paid out of a large sale. As the sale of books in England is not large, it might be necessary to allow him two dollars each; but even this would still leave nine dollars to be accounted for. Where does all this go? Part of it to the Chancellor of the Exchequer, part to the "Times," and other newspapers and journals that charge monopoly prices for the privilege of advertising, and the balance to the booksellers who "possess copyrights," and "sell their books at such exorbitant prices" that they have driven the government to turn bookseller, with a view to bring down prices; and these are the very men to whom it is now proposed to grant unlimited control over the sale of all books produced abroad.

It will, perhaps, be said that the treaty contains a proviso that the author shall sell his copyright to an American publisher, or shall himself cause his book to be republished here. Such a proviso may be there, but whether it is so, or not, no one knows, for every thing connected with this effort to extend the Executive power is kept as profoundly secret as were the arrangements for the Napoleonic coup d'etat of the 2d of December. Secrecy and prompt and decisive action are the characteristics of centralized governments—publicity and slow action those of decentralized ones. Admit, however, that such limitations be found in the treaty, by what right are they there? The basis of such a treaty is the absolute right of the author to his book; and if that be admitted, with what show of consistency or of justice can we undertake to dictate to him whether he shall sell or retain it— print it here or abroad? With none, as I think.

Admit, however, that he does print it, does the treaty require that the market shall always be supplied? Perhaps it does, but most probably it does not. If it does, does it also provide for the appointment of commissioners to see that the provision is always complied with? If it does not, nothing would seem to be easier than to send out the plates of a large book, print off a small edition, and by thus complying with the letter of the law, establishing the copyright for the long term of forty-two years, the moment after which the plates could be returned to the place whence they came, and from that place the consumers could be supplied on condition of paying largely to the Chancellor of the Exchequer, to the "Times," to the profits of Mr. Dickens' advertising sheet, to the author, to the London bookseller, to his agent in America, and the retail dealer here. In cases like this, and they would be numerous, the "few cents" would probably rise to be many dollars; and no way can, I think, be devised to prevent their occurrence, except to take one more step forward in centralization by the appointment of commissioners in various parts of the Union, to see that the market is properly supplied, and that the books offered for sale have been actually printed on this side of the Atlantic.

If the treaty does provide for publication here, it probably allows some time therefor, say one, two, or three months. It is, however, well-known that of very many books the first few weeks' sales constitute so important a part of the whole that were the publisher here deprived of them, the book would never be republished. No one could venture to print until the time had elapsed, and by that time the English publisher would so well have occupied the ground with the foreign edition that publication here would be effectually stopped. Even under the present ad valorem system of duties this is being done to a great extent. One, two, or three hundred copies of large works are cheaply furnished, and the market is thus just so far occupied as to forbid the printing of an edition of one or more thousands—to the material injury of paper-makers, printers, and book-binders, and without any corresponding benefit to the foreign author. Under the proposed system this would be done to a great extent.

Admit, however, that the spirit of the law be fully complied with, and let us see its effects. Mr. Dickens sells his book in England for 21_s_. ($5.00); and he will, of course, desire to have for it here as large a price as it will bear. Looking at our prices for those books which are copyright and of which the sale is large, he finds that "Bleak House" contains four times as much as the "Reveries of a Bachelor," which sells for $1.25, and he will be most naturally led to suppose that $3 is a reasonable price. The number of copies of his book that has been supplied to American readers, through newspapers and magazines, is certainly not less than 250,000, and the average cost has not been' more than fifty cents, giving for the whole the sum of
$125,000
To supply the same number at his price would cost.
750,000
Difference
$625,000
Of Mr. Bulwer's last work, the number that has been supplied to American consumers is probably but about two thirds as great, and the difference might not amount to more than
$350,000
Mr. Macaulay would not be willing to sell his book more cheaply than that of Mr. Bancroft's is sold, or $2 per volume, and he might ask $2.50. Taking it at the former price, the 125,000 copies that have been sold would cost the consumer $500,000
They have been supplied for
100,000
The difference would be
$400,000
Mr. Alison's work would make twelve such volumes as those of Mr. Bancroft, and his price would not be less than $25. The sale has amounted, as I understand, to 25,000 copies, which would give as the cost of the whole
$625,000
The price at which they have been sold is $5, giving
125,000
Difference
$500,000
Of "Jane Eyre" there have been sold 80,000, and if the price had been

similar to that of "Fanny Fern," they would have cost the consumers.
$100,000
They have cost about
25,000
Difference
$75,000
Total result of a "few cents" on five books, $1,950,000

Under the system of international copyright, one of two things must be done—either the people must be taxed in the whole of this amount for the benefit of the various persons, abroad and at home, who are now to be invested with the monopoly power, or they must largely diminish their purchases of literary food.

The quantity of books above given cannot be regarded as more than one twentieth of the total quantity of new ones annually printed. Admit, however, that the total were but ten times greater, and that the differences were but one fourth as great, it would be required that this sum of $1,950,000 should be multiplied two and a half times, and that would give about five millions of dollars; which, added to the sum already obtained, would make seven millions per annum; and yet we have arrived only at the commencement of the operation. All these books would require to be reprinted in the next year, and the next, and so on, and for the long period of forty-two years the payment on old books would require to be added to those on new ones, until the sum would become a very startling one. To enable us to ascertain what it must become, let us see what it would now be had this system existed in the past. Every one of Scott's novels would still be copyright, and such would be the case with Byron's poems, and with all other books that have been printed in the last forty-two years, of which the annual sale now amounts to many millions of volumes. To the present price of these let us add the charge of the author, and the monopoly charges of the English and American publishers, and it will be found quite easy to obtain a further sum of five millions, which, added to that already obtained, would make twelve millions per annum, or enough to give to one in every four thousand males in the United Kingdom, between the ages of twenty and sixty, a salary far exceeding that of our Secretaries of State. Let this treaty be confirmed, and let the consumption of foreign works continue at its present rate, and payment of this sum must be made. We can escape its payment only on condition of foregoing consumption of the books.

The real cause of difficulty is not to be found in "the few cents" required for the author, but in the means required to be adopted for their collection. Everybody that reads "Bleak House," or "Oliver Twist," would gladly pay their author some cents, however unwilling he might be to pay dollars, or pounds. So, too, everybody who uses chloroform would willingly pay something to its discoverer; and every one who believes in and profits by homeopathic medicines would be pleased to contribute "a few cents" for the benefit of Hahnemann, his widow, or his children. A single cent paid by all who travel on steam vessels would make the family of Fulton one of the richest in the world; but how collect these "few cents"? Grant me a monopoly, says the author, and I will appoint an agent, who shall supply other agents with my books, and I will settle with him. Grant us a monopoly, say the representatives of Hahnemann, and we will grant licenses, throughout the Union, to numerous men who shall be authorized to practice homeopathically and collect our taxes. Were this experiment tried, it would be found that millions would be collected, out of which they would receive tens of thousands. Grant us a monopoly, might say the representatives of Fulton, and we will permit no vessels to be built without license from us, and our agents will collect "a few cents" from each passenger, by which we shall be enriched. So they might be; but for every cent that reached them the community would be taxed dollars in loss of time and comfort, and in extra charges. It is the monopoly privilege, and not the "few cents," that makes the difficulty.

We are, however, advised by the advocates of this treaty that English authors must be "required" to present their books in American "mode and dress," and that regard to their own interests will cause them to be presented "at MODERATE PRICES for general consumption." If, however, they have acted differently at home, why should they pursue this course here? That they have so acted, we have proof in the fact that the British government has just been forced to turn bookseller, with a view to restrain the owners of copyrights in the exercise of power. Who, again, is to determine what prices are really "moderate" ones? The authors? Will Mr. Macaulay consent that his books shall be sold for less than those of Mr. Bancroft or Mr. Prescott? Assuredly not. The bookseller, then? Will he not use his power in reference to foreign books precisely as he does now in regard to domestic ones? If he deems it now expedient to sell a 12mo volume for a dollar or a dollar and a quarter, is it probable that the ratification of this treaty will open his eyes to the fact that it would be better for him to sell Mr. Dickens's works at fifty cents than at three dollars? Scarcely so, as I think. It is now about thirty years since the "Sketch Book" was printed, and the cheapest edition that has yet been published sells for one dollar and twenty-five cents. "Jane Eyre" contains probably about the same quantity of matter, and sells for twenty-five cents. Of the latter, about 80,000 have been printed, costing the consumers $20,000; but if they were to purchase the same quantity of the former, they would pay for them $100,000; difference, $80,000. What, now, would become of this large sum? But little of it would reach the author; not more, probably, than $10,000. Of the remaining $70,000, some would go to printers, paper-makers, and bookbinders, and the balance would be distributed among the publisher, the trade-sale auctioneers, and the wholesale and retail dealers; the result being that the public would pay five dollars where the author received one, or perhaps the half of one. We have here the real cause of difficulty. The monopoly of copyright can be preserved only by connecting it with the monopoly of publication. Were it possible to say that whoever chose to publish the "Sketch Book" might do so, on paying to its author "a few cents," the difficulty of this double monopoly would be removed; but no author would consent to this, for he could have no certainty that his book might not be printed by unprincipled men, who would issue ten thousand while accounting to him for only a single thousand. To enable him to collect his dues, he must have a monopoly of publication.

It may be said that if he appropriate to his use any of the common property of which books are made up, and so misuse his privilege as to impose upon his readers the payment of too heavy a tax, other persons may use the same facts and ideas, and enter into competition with him. In no other case, however, than in those of the owners of patents and copyrights, where the public recognizes the existence of exclusive claim to any portion of the common property, does it permit the party to fix the price at which it may be sold. The right of eminent domain is common property. In virtue of it, the community takes possession of private property for public purposes, and frequently for the making of roads. Not unfrequently it delegates to private companies this power, but it always fixes the rate of charge to be made to persons who use the road. This is done even when general laws are passed authorizing all who please, on compliance with certain forms, to make roads to suit themselves. In such cases, limitation would seem to be unnecessary, as new roads could be made if the tolls on old ones were too high; and yet it is so well understood that the making of roads does carry with it monopoly power, that the rates of charge are always limited, and so limited as not to permit the road-makers to obtain a profit disproportioned to the amount of their investments. In the case of authors there can be no such limitation. They must have monopoly powers, and the law therefore very wisely limits the time within which they may be exercised, as in the other case it limits the price that may be charged. In France, the prices to be paid to dramatic authors are fixed by law, and all who pay may play; and if this could be done in regard to all literary productions, permitting all who paid to print, much of the difficulty relative to copyright would be removed; but this course of operation would be in direct opposition to the views of publishers who advocate this treaty on the ground that it would add to "the security and respectability of the trade." They would prefer to pay for the copyright of every foreign book, because it would bring with it monopoly prices and monopoly profits, both of which would need to be paid by the consumers of books. To the paper-maker, printer, and bookbinder, called upon to supply one thousand of a book for the few, where before they had supplied ten thousand for the many, it would be small consolation to know that they were thereby building up the fortunes of two or three large publishing houses that had obtained a monopoly of the business of republication, and were thus adding to the "security and respectability of the trade." As little would probably be derived from this source by the father of a family who found that he had now to pay five dollars for what before had cost but one, and must therefore endeavor to borrow, where before he had been accustomed to buy, the books required for the amusement and instruction of his children.

Our State of New Jersey levies a transit duty of eight cents per ton on all the merchandise that crosses it. Had the imposition of this tax been accompanied by a law permitting all who chose to make roads, no one would have complained of it, as it would have been little more than a fair tax on the property of the railroad and other companies. Unfortunately, however, the course was different. To the company that collected it was granted a monopoly of the power of transportation, and that power has been so used that while the State received but eight cents the transporters charged three, five, six, and eight dollars for work that should have been done for one. The position in which the authors are necessarily placed is precisely the one in which our State has voluntarily placed itself. To enable them to collect their dues, some person or persons must have a monopoly of publication, and they must and will collect five, ten, and often twenty dollars for every one that reaches the author. The Union would gain largely by paying into our treasury thrice the sum we receive for transit duty, on the simple condition that we abolished the monopoly of transportation; and it would gain far more largely by doing the same with foreign authors. If justice does really call upon us to pay them, our true course would be to do it directly from the Treasury, placing, if necessary, a million of dollars annually at the disposal of the British government, upon the simple condition that it releases us from all claim to the monopoly of publication. Such a release would be cheap, even at two millions; enough to give $4,000 a year to five hundred persons, and that number would certainly include all who can even fancy us under any obligation to them. My own impression is, that no such payment is required by justice, either as regards our own authors or foreign ones. Of the former, all can be and are well paid, who can produce books that the public are willing to read, and no law that could be made would secure payment to those who cannot. Their monopoly extends over a smaller number of persons than does the English one; and if the more than thirty millions of people who are subject to the latter cannot support their few writers, the cause of difficulty is to be found at home, and there must the remedy be applied. Nevertheless, by adopting the course suggested, we should certainly free ourselves from any necessity for choosing between the payment of many millions annually to authors and the men who stand between them and the public, on the one hand, and of dispensing largely with the purchase of books, on the other. If the nation must pay, the fewer persons through whose hands the money passes the smaller will be the cost to it, and the greater the gain to authors.

The ratification of the treaty would impose upon us a very large amount of taxation that must inevitably be paid either in money or in abstinence from intellectual nourishment; and our authors should be able to satisfy themselves that the advantage to them would bear some proportion to the loss inflicted upon others. Would it do so? I think not. On the contrary, they would find their condition greatly impaired. All publishers prefer copyright books, because, having a monopoly, they can charge monopoly profits. To obtain a copyright, they constantly pay considerable sums at home for editorship of foreign books; but from the moment that this treaty shall take effect, the necessity for doing this will cease, and thus will our literary men be deprived of one considerable source of profit. Again, literary labor in England is cheap, because of want of demand; but international copyright, by opening to it our vast market, will quicken the demand, and many more books will be produced, the authors of all of which will be competitors with our own, who will then possess no advantages over them. The rates of American authors will then fall precisely as those of the British ones will rise; and this result will be produced as certainly as the water in the upper chamber of a canal lock will fall as that in the lower one is made to rise. On one side of the Atlantic literary labor is well paid, and on the other it is badly paid. International copyright will establish a level; and how much reason our authors have to desire that it shall be established, I leave it for them to determine.

The direct tendency of the system now proposed will be found to be that of diminishing the domestic competition for the production of books, and increasing our dependence on foreigners for the means of amusement and instruction; and yet the confirmation of the treaty is urged on the ground that it will increase the first and diminish the last. If it would have this latter effect, it is singular that the authors of England should be so anxious for the measure as they are. It is not usual for men to seek to diminish the dependence of others on themselves.

These, however, are, as I think, but a small part of the inconveniences to which our authors are now proposing to subject themselves. They have at present a long period allowed them, during which they have an absolute monopoly of the particular forms of words they offer to the reading public; and this monopoly has, in a very few years, become so productive, that authorship offers perhaps larger profits than any other pursuit requiring the same amount of skill and capital. Twenty years hence, when the market shall be greatly increased, it may, and as I think will, become a question whether the monopoly has not been granted for too long a period, and many persons may then be found disposed to unite with Mr. Macaulay in the belief that the disadvantages of long periods preponderate so greatly over their advantages, as to make it proper to retrace in part our steps, limiting the monopoly to twenty-one years, or one half the present period. The inquiry may then come to be made, what is the present value of a monopoly of forty-two years, as compared with what would be paid for one of twenty-one years; and when it is found that, in nine hundred and ninety-nine cases out of a thousand, one will sell for exactly as much as the other, it will perhaps be decided that no reason exists for maintaining the present law, even if no change be now made. Suppose, however, the treaty to be confirmed, establishing the monopoly of foreigners in our market, and that the people who have been accustomed to consume largely of cheap literature now find themselves deprived of it, would not this tend to hasten the period at which the existing law would come under consideration? I cannot but think it would. The common school makes a great demand for school-books, and both make a great demand for newspapers. All of these combine to make a demand for cheap books among an immense and influential portion of our community, that cannot yet afford to pay $1.25 for "Fern Leaves" or for the "Reveries of a Bachelor," although they can well afford 25 cents for a number of "Harper's Magazine," or for "Jane Eyre." Let us now suppose that the novels of Dickens and Bulwer, the books of Miss Aguilar, and those of other authors with which they have been accustomed to supply themselves, should at once be raised to monopoly prices and thus placed beyond their reach, would it not produce inquiry into the cause, and would not the answer be that we had given English authors a monopoly in our market to enable our own to secure a monopoly in that of England? Would not the sufferers next inquire by what process this had been accomplished, seeing that the direct representatives of the people had always been so firmly opposed to it; and would not the answer be that the literary men of the two countries had formed a combination for the purpose of taxing the people of both; and that when they had failed to accomplish their object by means of legislation, they had induced the Executive to interpose and make a law in their favor, in defiance of the well-known will of the House of Representatives? Under such circumstances, would it be extraordinary if we should, within three years from the ratification of the treaty, see the commencement of an agitation for a change in the copyright system? It seems to me that it would not.

The time for the arrival of this agitation would probably be hastened by an extension of the system of centralization that would next be claimed; for the present measure can be regarded as little more than the entering wedge for others. France and England profit enormously by setting the fashions for the world. New patterns and new articles are invented that sell in the first season for treble or quadruple the price at which they are gladly supplied in the second; and it is by aid of the perpetual changes bf fashion that foreigners so much control our markets. Recently, our manufacturers have been enabled to reproduce many new articles in very short time, and this has tended greatly to reduce the profits of foreigners, who are of course dissatisfied. Copyrights are now granted in both those countries for new patterns, new forms of clothing, andc. andc., and our next step will be towards the arrangement of a treaty for, securing to the inventor of a print, or a new fashion of paletot, the monopoly of its production in our markets; and when the claim for this shall be made, it will be found to stand on precisely the same ground with that now made in behalf of the producers of books, and must be granted. The Frenchman will then have the exclusive right of supplying us with new mousselines de laine, and the Englishman with new carpets and new forms of earthenware; and we shall be told that that is the true mode of developing manufacturing and artistic skill among ourselves. How much farther the system may be carried it is difficult to tell, for, when we shall once have established the system of regulating foreign and domestic trade by treaty, the House of Representatives will scarcely be troubled with much discussion of such affairs. Extremes generally meet, and it will be extraordinary, if progress in that direction shall not be followed by progress in the other, until our authors shall, at length, become perfectly satisfied of the accuracy of Mr. Macaulay, when he told the British authors, then claiming an extension of their monopoly to sixty years, that "the wholesome copyright" already existing would "share in the disgrace and danger of the new copyright" they desired to create.[1] They could scarcely do better than study his speech at length. At present, they are ill-advised, and their best friends will be those senators who, like Mr. Macaulay, shall oppose their literary countrymen.

[Footnote 1: Macaulay's Speeches, vol. i. p. 403.]

Admitting, however, that the measure proposed should not in any manner endanger existing privileges, what would be the gain to our authors in obtaining the control of the British market, compared with what they would lose from surrendering the control of our own? In the former, the sale of books is certainly not large. Few have been more popular than Tupper's "Proverbial Philosophy," and the price has been, as I learn, only 7_s._, or $1,68. Nevertheless, a gentleman fully informed in regard to it assures me that in fifteen years the average sale has been but a thousand a year, or 15,000 in all.[2] Compare this with the sale of a larger number of the "Reveries of a Bachelor," or of thrice the quantity of "Fern Leaves," at but little lower prices, in the short period of six months, and it will be seen how inferior is the foreign market to the domestic one. Were it otherwise—were the market of Britain equal to our own—could it be that we should so rarely hear of her literary men, dependent on their own exertions, but as being poor and anxious for public employment? Were it otherwise, should we need now to be told of the "utter destitution" of the widow and children of Hogg, so widely known as author of "The Queen's Wake," and as "The Shepherd" of "Blackwood's Magazine?" Assuredly not. Had literary ability been there in the demand in which it now is here, he would have written thrice as much, would have been thrice as well paid, and would have provided abundantly for his widow and his children. Nevertheless, our authors desire to trade off this great market for the small one in which he shone and left his family to starve, and thus to make an exchange similar to that of Glaucus when he gave a suit of golden armor for one of brass.

[Footnote 2: The sale here has been 200,000, at an average price of 50 cents. Had it been copyright, the price would have been double, and the "few cents" would have made a difference on this single book of $100,000. The same gentleman to whom I am indebted for the above facts informs me that he has paid to the author of a 12mo volume of 200 pages more than $23,000, and could not now purchase the copyright for $10,000; that for another small 12mo volume he has paid $7,000, and Expects to pay as much more; that to a third author his payments for the year have been $2500, and are likely to continue at that rate for years to come; and that it would be easy to furnish other and numerous cases of similar kind.]

What, however, are the prospects for the future? Will the British market grow? It would seem not, for death and emigration are diminishing the population, and the people who remain are in a state of constant warfare with their employers, who promised "cheap food" that they might obtain "cheap labor," and now offer low wages in connection with high-priced corn and beef. The people who receive such wages cannot buy books. Hundreds of thousands of persons are now out "on strike," or are "locked out" by the gentlemen who advocate this "cheap labor" system; and the result of all this extraordinary cessation from labor can be none other than the continued growth of poverty, intemperance, and crime. The picture that is presented by that country is one of unceasing discord between the few and the many, in which the former always triumph; and a careful examination of it cannot result in leading us to expect an increase in the desire to purchase books, or in the ability to pay for them.

Having looked upon that picture, let our authors next look to the one now presented by this country, as compared with that which could have been offered forty, thirty, or even twenty years since, and to obtain aid in understanding the facts presented to their view, let them read the following extract from a speech recently delivered by Mr. Cobden:—

"You cannot point to an instance in America, where the people are more educated than they are here, of total cessation from labor by a whole community or town, given over, as it were, to desolation. When I came through Manchester the other day, I found many of the most influential of the manufacturing capitalists talking very carefully upon a report which had reached them from a gentleman who was selected by the government to go out to America, to report upon the great exhibition in New York. That gentleman was one of the most eminent mechanicians and machine-makers in Manchester, a man known in the scientific world, and appreciated by men of science, from the astronomer royal downwards. He has been over to America, to report upon the progress of manufactures and the state of the mechanical arts in the United States, and he has returned. No report from him to the government has yet been published. But it has oozed out in Manchester that he found in America a degree of intelligence amongst the manufacturing operatives, a state of things in the mechanical arts, which has convinced him that if we are to hold our own, if we are not to fall back in the rear of the race of nations we must educate our people to put them upon a level with the more educated artisans of the United States. We shall all have the opportunity of judging when that report is delivered; but sufficient has already oozed out to excite a great interest, and I might almost say some alarm."

Having done this, let them next ask themselves what have been the causes of the vast change in the relative positions of the two countries. Doing this, will not the answer be, common schools, cheap school-books, cheap newspapers, and cheap literature? Has not each and every one of these aided in making authors, and in creating a market for their products? Having thus laid the foundation of a great edifice, are we likely to stop in the erection of the walls? Having in so brief a period created a great market for literature, is it not certain that it must continue to grow with increased rapidity? Assuredly it is; and yet it is that vast market that our authors desire to barter for one in which Hood was permitted almost to starve, in which Leigh Hunt, Lady Morgan, Miss Mitford, Tennyson, and Sir Francis Head even now submit to the degradation of receiving the public charity to the extent of a hundred pounds a year! The law as it now exists, invites foreign authors to come and live among us, and participate in our advantages. The treaty offers to tax ourselves for the purpose of offering them a bounty upon staying at home and increasing their numbers and their competition with the well-paid literary labor of this country. Were Belgrave Square to make a treaty with Grub Street, providing that each should have a plate at the tables of the other, the population of the latter would probably grow as rapidly as the dinners of the former would decline in quality, and it might be well for our authors to reflect if such might not be the result of the treaty now proposed.

Its confirmation is, as I understand, urged on some senators on the ground that consistency requires it. Being in favor of protection elsewhere, they are told that it would be inconsistent to refuse it here. In reply to this, it might fairly be retorted that nearly all the supporters of international copyright are advocates of the system called, in England, Free Trade; and that it is quite inconsistent in them to advocate protection here. To do this would however be as unnecessary as it would be unphilosophical. Both are perfectly consistent. Protection to the farmer and planter in their efforts to draw the artisan to their side, looks to carrying out the doctrine of decentralization by the annihilation of the monopoly of manufactures established in Britain; and our present copyright system looks to the decentralization of literature by offering to all who shall come and live among us the same perfect protection that we give to our own authors. What is called free trade looks to the maintenance of the foreign monopoly for supplying us with cloth and iron; and international copyright looks to continuing the monopoly which Britain has so long enjoyed of furnishing us with books; and both tend towards centralization.

The rapid advance that has been made in literature and science is the result of the perfect protection afforded by decentralization. Every neighborhood collects taxes to be expended for purposes of education, and it is from among those who would not otherwise be educated, and who are thus protected in their efforts to obtain instruction, that we derive many of our most thoughtful and intelligent men, and our best authors. The advocates of free trade and international copyright are, to a great extent, disciples in that school in which it is taught that it is an unjust interference with the rights of property to compel the wealthy to contribute to education of the poor. Common schools, and a belief in the duty of protection, are generally found together. Decentralization, by the production of local interests, protects the poor printer in his efforts to establish a country newspaper, and thus affords to young writers of the neighborhood the means of coming before the world. Decentralization next raises money for the establishment of colleges in every part of the Union, and thus protects the poor but ambitious student in his efforts to obtain higher instruction than can be afforded by the common school. Decentralization next protects him in the manufacture of school-books, by creating a large market for the productions of his pen, very much of which is paid for out of the product of taxes the justice of which is denied by those who advocate the British policy. Rising to the dignity of author of books for the perusal of already instructed men and women he finds himself protected by an absolute monopoly, having for its object to enable him to provide for himself, his wife, and his children. Of all the people of the Union, none enjoy such perfect protection as those connected with literature; yet many of them oppose protection to all others, while actively engaged in enlarging and extending the monopoly they themselves enjoy. It will scarcely answer for them to charge inconsistency on others.

How far the protection already granted has favored the development of literary tendencies, may be judged after looking to the single case of dramatic writers, who are not protected against representation without their consent; and, as that is their mode of publication, it follows that they do not enjoy the advantages granted to other authors. The consequence is, that we make so little progress in that department of literature, while advancing rapidly in every other. Permit me, my dear sir, to suggest that this is a matter worthy of your attention. There would seem to be no good reason for refusing to one class of authors what we grant so freely to all others.

Whether or not I shall have convinced you that international copyright should not be established, I cannot say, but I feel quite safe in believing that you must be convinced it is a question which requires to be publicly and fully discussed before we adopt any action looking in that direction. It is not a case of urgency. If the treaty be not confirmed, the only inconvenience to the authors will be delay, and this should be afforded, were it only to enable them to reflect at leisure upon the probable consequences of the measure in aid of which they have invoked the Executive power. Should they continue to believe their interests likely to be promoted by the adoption of such a measure as that which has been so pertinaciously urged the doors of Congress will always be open to them, and justice, though it may be delayed, will assuredly be done. Let them proceed in a constitutional way, and then, should their desires be gratified, they will have the satisfaction of knowing that their rights have been admitted after full and fair discussion before the people. Should they now succeed in obtaining, in secret session, the confirmation of a treaty negotiated in private, and in haste, they will, I think, "repent at leisure;" but repentance may, and probably will, come too late. The mischief will then have been done.

Having now, my dear sir, to the best of my ability, complied with your request, I remain,

Yours, very respectfully,

HENRY C. CAREY. Burlington, Nov. 28, 1853.

Hon. James Cooper.

NOTE

December 31, 1867.

Mr. Dickens's tale of "No Thoroughfare" is now being reprinted here in daily and weekly journals, and to such extent as to warrant the belief that the number in the hands of readers of the Union, will speedily exceed a million; obtained, too, at a cost so small as scarcely to admit of calculation. Under a system of International Copyright a similar number would, at the least, have cost $500,000. At 50 cents, however, the sale would not have exceeded 50,000, yielding to author and publisher probably $10,000. Would it be now expedient that, to enable these latter to divide among themselves this small amount, the former should tax themselves in one so greatly larger? Would it be right or proper that they should so do in the hope that American novelists and poets-should in like manner be enabled to tax the British people? Outside of the class of gentlemen who live by the use of their pens, there are few who, having examined the question, would, it is believed, be disposed to give to these questions an affirmative reply.

Of all living authors there is none that, in his various capacities of author, editor, and lecturer, is, in both money and fame, so largely paid as Mr. Dickens. That he and others are not doubly so is due to the fact that British policy, from before the days of Adam Smith, has tended uniformly to the division of society, at home and abroad, into two great classes, the very poor becoming daily more widely separated from the very rich, and daily more and more unfitted for giving support to British authors. That the reader may understand this fully, let him turn to recent British journals and study the accounts there given of "an agricultural gang system," whose horrors, as they tell their readers, "make the British West Indies almost an Arcadia" when compared with many of the home districts. Next, let him study in the "Spectator," now but a fortnight old, the condition of the

630,000 wretched people inhabiting Eastern London; and especially that of the 70,000 mainly dependent on ship and engine building, "too poor to go afield for employment, too poor to emigrate, too poor to do any thing but die," and wholly dependent on a weekly allowance per house, of front twenty to forty cents and a loaf of bread; that allowance, wretched as it is, to be obtained only at the cost of "standing hours among crowds made brutal by misery and privation." Further, let him read in the same journal its description of the almost universal dishonesty which has resulted from a total repudiation of the idea that international morality could exist; and then determine for himself if, under a different system, Britain might not have made at home a market for her authors that would far more than have compensated for deprivation of that one they now so anxiously covet abroad.

Seeking further evidence in reference to this important question, let him then turn to the "North British Review" for the current month and study the social sores of Britain.

For more than a century she has been sowing the wind, carrying, and in the direct ratio of their connection with her, poverty and slavery into important countries of the earth. She is now only reaping the whirlwind. When her literary men shall have begun to teach her people this—when they shall have said to them that public immorality and private morality cannot co-exist—when they shall have commenced to repudiate the idea that the end sanctifies the means—then, but not till then, the time may, perhaps, have come for lecturing the world on the moral side of the question of International Copyright. To this moment, so far as the writer's memory serves him, no one of them has yet entered on the performance of this important work.

www.ingramcontent.com/pod-product-compliance
Lightning Source LLC
Chambersburg PA
CBHW070847180526
45168CB00002B/978